THIS BOOK
BELONGS TO

....

....

I can't tell you how grateful I am that you decided to read my book. My most heartfelt thanks that you took time out of your life to choose my work and I hope you find benefit within these pages.

There are so many books available today that offer similar content so that makes it even more humbling that you decided to buying mine.

Tell me what you thought! I am eager to hear your opinion and ideas on what you read as are others who are looking for a good book to buy. Leave a review on Amazon.com so others can benefit from your wisdom!

With much thanks.

©COPYRIGHT 2024

The content contained within this book may not be reproduced, duplicated, or transmitted without direct written permission from the author or the publisher. Under no circumstances will any blame or legal responsibility be held against the publisher, or author, for any damages, reparation, or monetary loss due to the information contained within this book. Either directly or indirectly.

Legal Notice:
This book is copyright protected. This book is only for personal use. You cannot amend, distribute, sell, use, quote, or paraphrase any part, or the content within this book, without the consent of the author or publisher.

Disclaimer Notice:
Please note the information contained within this document is for educational and entertainment purposes only. All effort has been executed to present accurate, up-to-date, and reliable, complete information. No warranties of any kind are declared or implied. Readers acknowledge that the author is not engaging in the rendering of legal, financial, medical, or professional advice. The content within this book has been derived from various sources. Please consult a licensed professional before attempting any techniques outlined in this book. By reading this document, the reader agrees that under no circumstances is the author responsible for any losses, direct or indirect, which are incurred as a result of the use of the information contained within this document, including, but not limited to — errors, omissions, or inaccuracies.

Table of Contents

Part I : What's This Book ?	5
Part II : What's the Job ?	10
Section III : How to Start	25
Section IV : How to get input	36
Section VI : Working With Engineers	61
Section VII : Roadmaps and Release Plans	74
Section IX : Working With Customers	89
Section X : Working with the C - Suite	98
Section XI : General Good Things to Know	105
Section XII : Types of Deliverables	122
Section XIII : The End is just The Beginning	130

Part I: What's This Book?

What I hope you get out of this

5 seconds- Think of this as a quick start guide. It's what I wish I had when I started out in product management.

My entry into Product Management was not smooth or intentional. I envy those of you who know what you want and are making conscious strides to get there. I made a lot of mistakes. I didn't know what I was getting myself into. I got lucky in many respects. I've built products. I've launched products. I've end-of-life'd products. I'm not suggesting I've done it all, but I've done a decent amount.

What you're about to read is a list of some of the things I wish I knew back when I started out as a Product Manager. This is not all inclusive. I make no assumptions that this is complete. As a matter of fact, I can think of quite a few books & resources you should go look at first. But you're here now, so may as well get something out of this.

Think of this like a quick start guide. It's not the full instruction manual. It's what I would have liked to have read back when I started. It's a jumping off point. Sometimes all you need is a general pointer in the right direction. I hope this can serve as that pointer for you.

I'll let you in on a little secret. For things like Product Management, Relationships, and Parenting, there is no instruction manual. You will never find that one single 'how to' guide that removes your need to think in the moment and to make hard decisions. There's no playbook. At best, you can learn some terminology. You can learn some general themes. The rest is up to you.

If there's one thing I've learned in my various careers, it's that no amount of telling can substitute for actually doing. If you're a parent, you know this. You can read all the books you want about sleep training, but nothing prepares you for waking up 3 or 4 times in the middle of the night to calm a crying baby. Yes, you can intellectualize what that experience may be like, but unless you've done it, you don't know the feeling of fear and dread that seeps into your head after a month of this when you wonder if you will ever feel rested again. But just because reading can't fully prepare you, I know that for me and my wife, reading books on sleep training was invaluable. It gave us something to hold on to. We had a framework. We didn't feel we were completely twisting in the wind. When we were delirious with lack of sleep, we could fall back to the *Happiest Baby on the Block* and keep trying.

Product Management is much the same. No amount of reading can prepare you for the uncomfortable call where a customer berates you before cancelling their contract. No amount of thinking can get you through an internal stakeholder call where each person has their own opinion on what's most important and you have to figure out what to do with all the conflicting information. There's no course you can take to know how to communicate effectively with engineers. Product Management is a full contact sport. You have to get in there and do it.

But you know what?

The fact that you're trying makes all the difference.

There's research out there that says parenting books can harm your ability to parent (https://www.theatlantic.com/family/archive/2019/01/parenting-books-improv/580795/). The take-home message there is that parenting books can lead to increased stress because we're adding pressure to ourselves to be the perfect parents described in the book. In reality, we're all winging it. If I look hard, I *may* be able to find a parallel with Product Management. Don't add pressure to yourself to be perfect.

I'm firmly in the camp of learning from other's mistakes and giving yourself plenty of latitude to make your own.

Figure out what works for you. Make mistakes. Try. Fail. Try again. You won't be perfect. Don't try to be perfect. Just try.

Hopefully you can learn from my mistakes.

A good friend of mine once told me that other people's advice is not what's best for you. It's what they think would have been best for them.

Keep that in mind while reading this book. This is what I wish I had known. Maybe someday, you'll have your own list of things you'd wish you'd known. If so, I look forward to reading it.

What this book is not

5 Seconds- This book is not about how to get into product management. This book is for new PM's and is the advice I wish I had.

There's an incredible amount of information on the internet and in books on how to become a product manager. There's guides on how to edge your way in. How to network. How to interview. How to start doing PM work even before you're officially a product manager so that you can get the next open PM position.

This book is not one of those.

You're not going to find any advice on how to get hired as a PM. You're not going to get interview tips.

I'm assuming that you're already a PM. I assume you have the job.

I'm also assuming that you're in a "product" organization. That means you're in a place that values what PM's bring to the table. You're likely not their first product manager. You're working with other PM's senior to you.

This book also isn't graduate school level stuff. There's a whole world of books and blogs to help you become a world-class product manager. But those concepts are so far away from where new PM's are in their career. If you've been a PM for 2, 3, or 4 years, you've already learned most of this. If you're just starting out or you're thinking of becoming a PM and want to get a sense of what it's like, then this book is for you. It won't help you become a PM, but it just may help you be a better one.

Structure of the book

5 Seconds- The book is split into big topics, each with multiple smaller essays. Each of these is prefaced with a 5 second synopsis.

First, this book is meant to be read in any order you like. It's a quick start guide and you're welcome to jump to any section you'd like to learn about. I tried to organize this into larger themes, each with smaller essays under each main category. You can think of the categories as chapters if you like.

The 5 second synopsis..., you'll read more about that later, but I believe that it's crucial to both your thinking and communication skills that you're able to condense the essence of an argument or position into a five second explanation. You should know what you're getting into before reading a long-winded diatribe. Read the 5 Seconds section and decide if the following information is worth your time.

Part II: What's the Job?

Judgment

5 Second Summary- Product Management is first and foremost about your judgment.

What is the job of a product manager? You can't code. You can't sell. You don't balance the books. You don't pay the bills. You get in the way. So why do they hire you? Why does a company spend the money to bring in someone with few tangible skills?

It's because of your judgment.

Judgment is the most critical aspect of your job.

You may hear that it's communication skills. Those are important as well, but it's your judgment that will help you know *what* to communicate to each stakeholder group. It's your judgment that will tell you when something is off and you need to wrangle people across multiple teams.

Judgment is how to know when to tell the CEO "I know you want that feature, but we have bigger fish to fry" and when to realize that the CEO is spot on and that you need to take that new input and alter your roadmap.

Judgment is how you can take all the various demands put on you and know which is the most important. You'll have various stakeholders, each with their own list of demands that are rarely aligned with each other. You have to listen through the ask to get to the why of it all.

No amount of coding experience can prepare you for that. No amount of selling experience can either. You may be the best communicator of all time, but if your judgment is off, all you'll be able to do is convince people to go in the wrong direction.

So how do you gain judgment?

It's gained by experience. It's gained by making hard decisions and learning from them. You can learn from good decisions. Look back and figure out what you did and why the decision was the right one. Try to replicate that process. You can learn from bad decisions. Look back and figure out what you did wrong and why the decision was the wrong one. But here's the key… you have to make the decisions in the first place. The worst thing you can do is to make no decisions at all. That's the cowardly way out and you'll soon be looking for another line of work.

Influence without authority

5 Second- You have no direct authority, but still need to convince, coerce and cajole others to do what you think is best. Hint- that's basic leadership.

This topic gets a lot of attention. As a Product Manager, you don't have any direct reports. The engineers you work with typically report to an Engineering Manager who often reports to a VP of Engineering, or some other Manager of Engineering Managers. You can't hire, fire, or discipline anyone in your company. You are an IC, an Individual Contributor. How can you be expected to get anything done?

Here's a hint: being an effective leader is the same whether or not people officially report to you.

Being able to effectively lead people in the direction you want is done the same way whether or not there's a line between you on the org chart. Product Managers need to gain the trust of the people on their teams. So do all other managers. The line "because I told you to" is a tool of last resort that can only be used a couple of times before it loses its effectiveness. If you're a parent, you know this. Your children 'report' to you in many respects, but if you rely on that as a means of influencing behavior, you'll win many battles, but will likely lose the war. You get kids to do what you want them to do by getting them to *want* to please you. It's the same with the people you work with.

Individual contributors at all levels of an organization can lead and influence regardless of the official structure of the org chart.

There's too much literature in the Product Management community about influencing without authority. That's not the real issue. The real issue is how to influence *with* authority without *using* the authority. If you can do that, it doesn't matter if you have authority or not.

If you want to influence, be a better leader. Study leadership principles and apply them. It doesn't matter that no one reports to you. The definition of a leader is that people follow them. That's it. Don't make too big of a deal about not having authority. Go lead instead.

No typical way in

5 Seconds- There's no 'right' path to product. You will feel out of place.

Before becoming a product manager, I was a Navy submarine officer. There were three very straightforward paths to being a submarine officer: 1) go to the Naval Academy, graduate & get placed on a submarine, 2) go through ROTC at another school, graduate & get placed on a submarine, or 3) graduate college, go through Officer Candidate School for 12 weeks, get placed on a submarine. The paths to a submarine are clear and repeatable.

After leaving the Navy, I joined ExxonMobil as a drilling engineer. Everyone there had a similar path in. Go to college, get a degree (usually in petroleum engineering like I did), graduate, join ExxonMobil.

Most career paths are similar. There's a fairly repeatable pattern people make before starting certain jobs.

That's not the case with product management.

I've never met two people in the world of product that had the same route into this career.

It's almost a badge of honor talking about how you backed into this role. How you were doing one thing and the company needed you to help with some project or design work and you happily got sucked into this world. How you were an engineer and became the go-to person to help with feature design and then a spot opened up for a PM role and you took it. How you went from the military, to oil and gas to being a financial advisor (yes, I did that too), before going and getting an MBA and elbowing your way into a software startup that decided to pivot three months after you joined.

My wife is a Senior Product Manager. She earned her Chemical Engineering degree and went to work for Samsung making semiconductors. A very traditional career path. A few years later she decided to throw caution to the wind and signed up for a coding bootcamp. She got hired on as a Ruby on Rails developer at a tiny company. Two years later, she applied to be a PM at a healthcare company and got the job. She's been promoted multiple times and recently changed companies. Her path is uncommon, but at the same time, it's the same story as everyone else has. It's the same story I have. Do one thing, do it well and then realize you're hearing the siren song of Product Management.

Here's the ugly secret...

You will have imposter syndrome. Expect it. Embrace it. Don't fight it. Accept it and realize it means you want to be better. That's a good thing.

There's no certificate saying you're ready for the job. There *are* certificates & courses, but they prepare you for this job in the same way that reading a book prepares you to play football.

Distill it to 5 seconds or less

5 Seconds- You need to be able to explain it in 5 seconds or less.

Since you're often in meetings with executives with hectic schedules and dozens of other issues they're dealing with, you need to have the ability to boil down your message into sound-bites.

When I was first starting out in my PM career, my boss would ask me a question and I'd over explain. Typically, it was because I wanted to impress her by showing how much I knew or because I didn't know the information well enough, so I'd try to bluff her. Either way, I'd go into some long winded explanation. I'd give background, I'd give nuance, I'd give edge-cases. In reality, I'd ramble. She'd stop me and say "I need to be able to understand this in 5 seconds or less".

There's a scene in the opening of "A River Runs Through It" where the father is having his son write a paper. The son brings the draft and the dad played by Tom Skerrit says "Half as long" each time the son brings a new draft. (https://www.youtube.com/watch?v=36-VQQawpsk). I saw the movie in highschool, but didn't appreciate this scene until I had this job. My first year as a PM was much like this.

Brevity forces clarity of thought. It forces deeper understanding of the issue at hand and requires empathy for the listener. What does your audience need to know to understand the issue? What elements are critical and what can be left out?

My boss would inevitably ask questions after I learned how to give 5 second explanations, but because I had spent the time to think and probe the issue beforehand, I was better equipped to answer the follow-on questions.

Obviously, not *everything* can be boiled down to 5 seconds or less, but chances are, you're spending more time explaining than you should be.

Product Management is a Full Contact Job

5 Seconds- You can't learn product management in a book or class. You have to learn by doing.

There's an incredible amount of resources for product managers and aspiring product managers nowadays. There's books. There's online courses. There's in-person training (although I suspect the 2020 lockdown has put a damper on those).

My point is that if you want to read about product management, you definitely can. You're obviously doing it now and I for one think that's just wonderful!

Here's the dirty little secret though: product management is a full contact sport and you don't learn how to do a full contact sport by reading about it.

Yes, you read to learn the rules. You attend a class to learn the players and positions. You attend a Meet-up to hear war stories from others.

But the real learning comes from doing.

No book can tell you how to set reasonable expectations to your sales team. No 30 minute exercise in a two day class can prepare you for dealing with a customer that's threatening to leave because your product doesn't do what they want it to do.

These are skills you learn by doing. By getting on the field and getting knocked down and getting back up again. I think that's why so many PM's come from such varied backgrounds. You should have this sort of experience before becoming a PM.

I guess this is my way of saying to not be afraid of starting out as a PM. There's often a tendency to think "I need to be certified to be a PM" or "I need this course in order to ask for a transfer into the PM department". I don't think that's necessary.

Later in this book, I'll talk more about how to get started. Yes, there is some reading involved, but it's not as much as you think.

Remember, if you want to learn to be a boxer, you get in the ring and box. If you want to be a football player, you put on your pads and get on the field. If you want to be a product manager, do the things that product managers do. Don't just read about them. But keep reading this book.

You want (some) angry customers

5 Second- An angry customer means your product is important to them. If it wasn't, they wouldn't be angry, they'd just leave.

Don't get me wrong, you don't want *all* your customers to be angry, but if you don't have *any* angry customers, you've got to ask yourself if you've got a product people really need.

You know why internet service providers have such horrible customer service? Because they can.

The Internet is a necessity for most households. Especially during the Covid lockdown. You'd think companies would be scrambling to have the best service, the best products on the market...you know *competing* for your business. Instead, you have one, maybe two choices for your internet service provider. So you call them up. You yell, you threaten to leave. They kindly ignore you because they know there's some other schmuck yelling at the only other ISP in town threatening to switch to your ISP. They have a product their customer base *needs*. You can only be so lucky.

I'm not suggesting you treat your customers like the cable companies do. That's just crazy and just a little bit evil. What I'm saying is that the ISP's have a product people want. You want to be in that position.

When you get an angry customer, embrace it. Revel in it. Realize that it means you have something that people need, not just want. I once heard that reported defects are love letters from your customers. They've taken the time out of their day to tell you how to improve your product.

All this said, you still want and need raving customers who are willing to recommend your product on the record. You need advocates in the marketplace. But if there's nothing unique about what you're building and very low switching costs, you'll never hear from these angry customers...and that's a red flag. As the Lumineers said "The opposite of love's indifference."

It's not Project Management

5 Second- Product Management and Project Management sound similar, but are very different jobs…even if you need some project management skills.

If you're just starting out in this field, you may get confused by these two titles. They sound similar, but so do the football positions of Quarterback and Cornerback. There's a bit of a superiority complex on each side and it's well deserved…on each side. Neither role is better, but they are quite different. Let's go into a bit of history to explain.

Imagine building a massive infrastructure project like a bridge or a dam. How do you schedule out all the work? How do you know when to plan for the next shipment of materials? How do you know when you've reached the definition of done? Enter the Gantt chart. Named for Henry Gantt, these charts are wonderful planning tools for *project* planning. Gantt's processes & techniques focused on getting various groups of people together to work towards a common goal that would eventually have a finish line. Let's build a dam. Let's erect a skyscraper. You had to know what the end goal was before you started. You had to have a timeline to know when to order supplies. There were gates & milestones to pass in order to hand off to the next team. Everything had to wrap up on time for the ribbon cutting ceremony and if things were running late, you needed to know *how* late.

That's how software used to be built. First you figured out what the software should do and documented the requirements. Then the project got handed off to another team who took the requirements and documented the features the engineers would build. Then engineering read the features and started coding. Then they were done and handed the code over to the quality team who checked for bugs and defects. The code was bundled up on floppy drives or some other media, wrapped in a cardboard box, shrink wrapped and put on the shelf at your local computer software store. That's if the software was for personal use. A lot of software is built for companies to use internally and is never sold commercially, but that's another topic.

This sort of software development process is called Waterfall.

The person or persons in charge of this choreographed dance are *project* managers. There's a start, a middle and an end to these projects.

That's not you. You're a *product* manager.

What we figured out over the past 30 years of building software, especially now that so much of it is running in the cloud and is never boxed up and shrink wrapped, is that products need to continually evolve. There's no way to know ahead of time what all the requirements are going to be. You can't craft all the features, put them on a Gantt chart and schedule them out for two years and have any hope that you're going to deliver something the market wants.

There will be times in your job when you may need to act like a mini-project manager. If you're about to release a brand new product to the market, there *will be* a finish line for the launch. Someone will need to coordinate marketing efforts, sales enablement, customer education, pricing, etc. You may be tapped for that effort, or your company may assign someone else as the project manager for this work. But remember, when running a product launch, the "launch" is the project. The product management piece is an ongoing effort that continues before, during and after the project is over.

At larger companies, a project manager may work across multiple products to keep timelines and wrangle various departments. At smaller companies, the project management work may be only part of one person's job.

Again, one role isn't better than the other, but they're very different so don't be confused by similar sounding names.

Section III: How to Start

5 Seconds: I can't tell you what you ultimately need to do, but these are some ways you can accelerate your progress.

So much of your reputation in a job is formed in the first few months you're there. Starting off with a good impression will carry you far. It's so much harder to overcome people's perceptions of you that it's worth putting in the effort early.

Get in the way

5 Seconds- You *will* slow things down, but you need to get in the way. It's the only way to learn.

I used to be in the Navy. The day I reported to my submarine, the ship was getting ready to get underway. The transition from a ship tied to the pier to a ship in the open ocean is quite an operation. Everyone on the ship had a role to play...except me.

I was in the way.

Everywhere I stood, I was in the way. Wherever I was, someone else needed to be there.

It was like that for months.

Until slowly, I wasn't so much in the way. I had my little part, but I was still new and unsure of myself, so I was still in the way, but not as much as before.

Then one day, I started realizing that other people were in *my* way. I knew what needed to be done. I knew my role. That's when I knew I was pulling my own weight.

Starting out as a product manager is much the same.

You're in meetings where you don't have context and conversations hinge on unstated assumptions. Terms are used that are loaded with meanings that are hidden from you. You have two options. Option one, stay out of the way. Let the flow of information go around you. Don't block traffic. Let the conversation run its course. Or...option two, get in the way. Ask questions, slow things down, not just to slow them down, but to make sure you're learning.

You need to get in the way.

Ask questions. During meetings. After meetings. Ask questions.

Keep a list of questions. Set up a 1-1 for the sole purpose of getting your questions answered. Personally, I use Microsoft Onenote and have a page for every person I have 1-1's with. If I have a question, I'd jot it down there and then during our next conversation, boom, I'd have the questions that I need right at my fingertips. You can use Evernote, Notion, Confluence, or any other tool you like, but I highly recommend this practice.

Your questions *will* slow things down. You'll be taking people's time. You'll force others to slow down.

Getting in the way early is the best way to get out of people's way tomorrow.

Accept the fact that you may frustrate people. Accept that you may be told "I don't have time now". Keep asking.

This is where you need to pull in your engineering manager. It's their job to get you up to speed. Use them instead of other engineers. The engineering manager should be protecting engineer's time and will have the bigger picture context to help you. Engineering managers have busy schedules, but they should realize that educating you on the nuances of the company and the product is an investment in the team's future.

The faster you learn the context of your company and product, the faster you can be a productive member of the team. Get over the worry of adding friction to a fast-moving organization. Any company worth joining understands the cost of onboarding a new team member. Their part of the bargain is to teach you. Your part of the bargain is to ask for that teaching. And keep asking. And keep asking.

Get in the way early and often. Before you know it, you'll find other people slowing you down asking you to explain the nuances of some complicated issue. You'll be getting asked questions after meetings. Remember how you felt when you joined and treat those people kindly.

You Can't Think Your Way Out of This

5 Seconds- You have to learn by doing. Reading is great, thinking is necessary, but *doing* is the glue that makes it stick.

When I was in 7th grade, I started wrestling. I was a gangly kid without any natural athletic ability. I wore my tortoise shell glasses with my singlet and wrestling shoes for my team picture. I remember thinking that wrestling was split into technique and strength. I didn't like the strength part of it. I thought "If I can have better technique, then it's ok if I'm not as strong as the other kids".

I tried to think my way out of getting stronger.

My wrestling career lasted two uneventful seasons.

Recently, I was on a call with my engineering manager and another peer of mine. We were talking about the effort required to transition from business hour support to 24x7 support. It's quite a change in mindset and requires the engineers to do things they're not used to doing. The engineering manager raised valid concern after valid concern and said "It's going to take us months to figure out what needs to be done before we can shift to 24x7 support." The other person on the call (who's team had been doing 24x7 for months) said, "You can't think your way out of this. You have to start and figure out where you fail. *That's* how you'll get better."

That quote stuck with me.

As Mike Tyson said "Everyone has a plan until they get hit in the face". We can plan all we want. The only way to improve is to get hit in the face...except maybe not by Mike Tyson.

When I started out as a product manager, I thought I could think my way out of the grunt work. I thought I could just be smarter than the other folks and I'd be ok. Just like in wrestling, I didn't think I needed to do the low-level, repetitive work needed to get stronger in the job.

I eventually learned what I failed to learn in wrestling. I can't think my way out of the hard work. I had to dig in. I had to do the tedious investigations. I needed to create readable documentation. I had to set the meetings and learn how to lead them. I had to have awkward conversations.

Only once I learned to embrace the grunt work, was I able to grow as a product manager. I had to learn to love the push-ups and sit-ups of the job. Well, maybe I never learned to *love* them, but at least I appreciate what they did for me.

Oh, and guess what? We got to full 24x7 support two months earlier than anticipated because we dove in and started. We stopped thinking and just did.

Assume your company knows what it's doing

5 Seconds- You don't know enough to change things immediately. Assume there's a good reason for the insanity you see around you.

When I started out as a PM I saw inefficiencies everywhere. There were manual processes that I thought needed to be automated. I tried to chunk my days like I had read about. I wanted to change things early. I remember standing up to the head of engineering after being at the company for two months with some principled issue about story points. It was pointless, pun intended.

I assumed early on that I knew the right way to work and that this place was doing it wrong. I suspect you'll do the same.

Start out assuming that your company is doing things the right way when taking into account its history and current situation. There may be a good reason for that painful manual process and you just don't know what it is.

I tried to make changes early. I failed. For a few reasons:

1. I didn't have the context. There were good and valid reasons why certain things were how they were. Processes and culture grow and evolve. Making change is hard, making change without knowing the history & context is near impossible.
2. I didn't have the social capital. I was the new guy on the block. Why would I know better than others who had worked here for years? I needed to gain the trust of the team before they would listen to my changes.

I would have been much better off assuming that *I* should be the one to change how I work. I would have assimilated better and been in a better position to understand why things were as they were.

At some point, you *will* be in a position to see the bigger picture. You will have ideas and recommendations for process & procedure changes that will benefit the organization. Once you're there, once other people are in your way and not the other way around, you'll be in a much better position to push for change.

The [5th Habit of Highly Effective People](#) is "First seek to understand, then to be understood".

I recommend reminding yourself of this as a new PM. First, do your best to understand what's going on, then dig in more to understand *why* things are as they are. Then you'll be in a much better place when you want others to understand you and what you want.

Get a towel. Read *Inspired* by Marty Cagan. Learn some vocabulary.

5 Second- Although Product Management is a full contact sport, you'll learn faster if you know some of the vocabulary.

I know I said that reading isn't the most important aspect of learning the job. I stand by that, but by reading a couple things (like what you're reading now) can jump start your journey. To be clear, the jump start is more about the vocabulary & terms you learn than about any real practical knowledge (this book included).

If you read one book on the topic of Product Management, make it *Inspired* by Marty Cagan. I have no affiliation with that book or author. I only wish I had read it earlier in my own career. The biggest take away is that it gives a framework to hang the practical experience you will gain over the first few years on the job. *Inspired* is a fully balanced meal with all the vitamins a healthy mind needs. Feel free to peruse Medium posts or LinkedIn articles, but at best, those are snacks. Sure, they may have a good point or two, but mostly they're fluff. Even if they're insightful, it's hard to refer back to them. Your likelihood of forgetting them is high. Go for the meaty book you can refer back to as you learn more.

The towel analogy comes from *The Hitchhiker's Guide to the Galaxy*.

> a towel has immense psychological value. For some reason, if a strag (strag: non-hitch hiker) discovers that a hitch hiker has his towel with him, he will automatically assume that he is also in possession of a toothbrush, face flannel, soap, tin of biscuits, flask, compass, map, ball of string, gnat spray, wet weather

gear, space suit etc., etc. Furthermore, the strag will then happily lend the hitch hiker any of these or a dozen other items that the hitch hiker might accidentally have "lost". What the strag will think is that any man who can hitch the length and breadth of the galaxy, rough it, slum it, struggle against terrible odds, win through, and still knows where his towel is is clearly a man to be reckoned with.

Your new vocabulary is your towel. If you know some key words and tricky phrases, people will be willing to lend you their knowledge.

Read *The First 90 Days*

5 Seconds- This is an evergreen book that you'll want to read again and again when starting a new job.

Most business and self-help books contain pithy bits of information that you can't really do much with. I'm reminded of an intentional misquote I saw years ago: "I am vast and contain platitudes". They feel good to read, but don't give much tangible advice.

The First 90 Days is the exact opposite.

It's meaty with very specific guidance on how to tackle the first three months of a new job. It has different advice depending on what kind of job you're taking on. It's more of a workbook than a motivational book. It's not one you read in bed. It's one you read with a notebook and pen to take notes and to make your plan.

Buy this book now.

Even if you've started in your job, buy the book and read it.

At some point you'll change jobs or get promoted. When that happens, read the book again.

This isn't a book on Product Management. It's a book on how to hit the ground running. Regardless of whether you stay in this career or move to something else, *The First 90 Days* should be on your bookshelf.

Section IV: How to get input

5 Second- The only way to know what to build next is to get input from everywhere. Don't innovate in a bubble.

In this section, we'll cover how to collect and sort out all the noise of people asking for this or that and how you can sift through that noise to hear the signal. My background is in B2B (business to business) products, so this may not be quite as applicable for a B2C (business to consumer) product manager. I'm sure some of the concepts and ideas will carry over.

The good news for you is that as a new product manager, you're not expected to come up with all the answers. Someone has built the vision. Someone has built the strategy. At the early stage of your career, your job is to execute. Just as a first year architect isn't designing Manhattan skyscrapers right out of college, you're not going to be responsible for designing a billion dollar application. You *will* be expected to own pieces and parts of it. And for those parts you're responsible for, you need to learn how to get the right level of input to make the right decisions.

Why over What

5 Second- Dig into the request to get at the 'why' of the ask. Everyone will tell you what they want. Few people will tell you why they want it.

If you're working on a product that has any user base at all, you're going to have feature requests. Users won't be shy about telling you what they want. The challenge you face is to understand why they want what they want. This is the 'faster horse' problem. To give people what they need, you have to understand why they need it.

There's an old saying that no one walks into a hardware store needing a drill bit. They walk into a hardware store with an "I need a hole" problem. I'd argue that this is only eliminating the first, most obvious assumption. It doesn't go far enough into the 'why'.

Assume you work at the hardware store and someone says to you: "I need a ¼" drill bit". You tell them they're on aisle 5 and even walk them over there. They pick out the first one they see and you assume everything is solved.

You're surprised when they return back later that day with a mangled bit asking for a refund. What happened?

You failed to ask "why do you need the drill bit?". In this scenario, it matters if they're drilling through sheetrock & wood studs or if they're drilling through cement.

Asking *why* cuts through assumptions. Customers and other stakeholders will assume you just know what's in their mind. If you're not careful, you'll assume they know what's in your mind. Asking *why?* gives permission to set aside those assumptions.

'Why do you need a ¼" hole?'

'Because I'm hanging pictures on my brick fireplace'
'Have you thought about brick clips? You may not need to make a permanent hole.'

'Why do you need a ¼" hole?'
'I stick this in the wall and hang my coat on it. I have another coat so I need a way to hang it.'
'So you don't need another bit. You need a hanger.'

I realize these are somewhat contrived examples, but you'd be surprised how often customers can ask for something without understanding they're asking for the solution when they should be giving you the problem.

And I won't even get into the cross-selling aspect. If someone is hanging pictures, it could be that they're redecorating, or just moved, or any of a dozen other activities, any one of which could require more of your services.

Knowing why someone wants something gives you options. There may be a better solution the customer hasn't thought of. There could be some other work-around that can satisfy them that doesn't take engineering effort, freeing your team to work on other, more critical features. Your job is to solve their problem, not to just be a ticket taker.

If you don't dig into the why, you'll always be in a reactive mode.

Types of Requests

5 Seconds- Some requests are nice to have's. Others hold the key to a multimillion dollar deal. It's critical to keep asking questions until you know you which is which.

Requests come in all forms. Some are simple and benign. Some may be blocker for a customer to sign a multi-year multi-million dollar deal. You need to know immediately which is which. While I'd love to say it's easy to tell the difference at face value by just reading the request, it's often not that simple. A nice to have for one customer may be the most important thing for another.

Customers paying annual subscriptions expect to have some input on your roadmap. This is especially true for B2B customers. You won't have as many customers, but those you do have are paying you more and so their needs represent a larger fraction of your business.

What are the different types of requests? And how can you ensure you know which is which?

We have three primary flavors of requests. This may not meet your exact needs, but it's not a bad framework to adapt.

Most requests are straightforward. Customer wants something. We ask that the customer-facing rep fill out a short form when they submit the request on the customer behalf.

There's the pain section. What's the pain the customer is currently experiencing? In here, we're getting to the 'why' of the problem.

There's the proposed solution. This is the 'what' section. This is where the customer and the customer-facing representative is able to propose an idea. It may not be what is ultimately implemented, but gives a chance for the customer to speak their peace on their desires.

We also ask the customer-representative to indicate how critical this request is. The wording may vary in your organization, but is this a Nice to Have, or a Really Important request? Beyond that, there's another lever that can be pulled.

If there's a feeling that the customer will not sign up or will not renew their license without this feature, we can assign the request as a Deal Breaking Request. Flagging a request like this helps it cut through the noise and brings focus to this particular need for this particular customer.

The product team is now in the position to make a business decision and is able to bring that decision to the C-suite. We know the value of the feature. With a little investigation, we can estimate the cost. We also ask for the value of the customer's business. Now we can compare costs & benefits.

Not every Deal Breaking Request is implemented, but they're all discussed openly. We don't want there to be any surprise if we lose a customer due to not implementing their request. Getting everyone on the same boat is vital and this is just one way we try to do that.

It took time for the product organization to decide on the right way to ask for this information and even longer for us to get the rest of the company onboard with the process, but it was time and energy well spent. There's a clear way to ask for normal things and a clear way to raise a red flag and bring attention to something that's more important than the typical request.

Small group sessions

5 Seconds- Everyone has their own perspectives. It's useful to get different perspectives in the same room and let the ideas fight it out.

Your company will have a few different departments, each with various stakeholders who want to pull you in their own direction. Pre-Sales will want the product to demo better. Support will want more troubleshooting features that customers will rarely ever see. Sales will want whatever the next customer is specifically asking for. Marketing will want whatever will help them in their analyst conversations. Your job is to balance all these competing needs.

How do you do that?

One way is to have regular 1-1's with these stakeholders to dig into their needs. I highly recommend doing this. The challenge with this approach is that you'll likely get a bunch of top-10 lists with little to no overlap. Even after pushing for the 'why' of each top-10 list, you'll still get multiple, good and valid 'whys'.

Worse, if you don't deliver for one group, they'll feel slighted and rejected. For example, if you decide that the most important thing is to sign new customers and get them on boarded at whatever cost, you may decide to underinvest in work to make your Support team happy. Without good communication, your Support team may not understand why they're not getting the tools & features needed to help active customers.

Here's one solution that can help. Set a monthly meeting with key stakeholders from various departments to review the top needs of each department.

This does a few things for everyone involved.

You hear the different perspectives all at once. This helps combat the "last-in, first-out" problem where the last good idea you hear is the first one you work on.

Key stakeholders feel that their voices are heard. While this may sound like it's pacifying people, it's so very important that people feel heard. As a product manager, you have to ensure that people don't feel shut down and keeping an open line of communication is part of your job.

Key stakeholders hear the *other* priorities. Being a product manager is like living as the hub of a wagon wheel. You're connected to the outer rim by many different spokes. You hear what everyone wants. Few other departments have this privilege. Most know what they want & need and *may* tangentially understand some of the needs of other departments, but often only at a superficial level. These cross-team meetings will educate stakeholders and help them see that while you're not working to solve *their* specific problems, you are working to make the product better for customers and ultimately, your company.

If you play your cards right, you can turn the meeting attendees into advocates for you and your team. The attendees can report back to their departments with the *why* of what Product is building. They may not love the answer, but at least they'll understand the reason.

Customer Calls

5 Seconds- Bypass the middleman and talk directly to customers, but be careful, they don't know what they're asking for.

You build the product for customers, right? So why not get feedback & input directly from them? They're the ones with the checkbook. They're the reason you're employed. Isn't it better to talk directly to them instead of other internal stakeholders who may each have their own agenda?

Why, yes, that's absolutely right. Getting in front of customers and hearing directly from them is hugely beneficial.

They have no agenda other than to further their own needs. They're typically very up front about that. Your roadmap & product plans are not interesting to them unless those plans dovetail with their own plans.

Here's the challenge with customers…they don't know what they need, but they know exactly what they want. Be careful about becoming a note-taker during customer calls. You'll be so busy taking notes, you'll forget to push back and dig into the *why*. There's that pesky 'why' word again.

Also, customers forget that you haven't been indoctrinated into their acronym culture. You have your own acronyms that you need to be careful using, but since the customer is paying you, they typically don't have those same concerns. Remember the drill & hole analogy? Customers will tell you they're building a pergola and you may never have heard of a pergola. They may tell you they're building a temporary external asset overflow container (i.e. storage shed) and you have to learn how to figure out whether this is some special type of structure that has unique needs or whether this has the same sort of construction concerns that most any other outdoor structure has. You have to be able to ask enough questions to get the right level of understanding while still being ok with some uncertainty about the aspects of their needs that are outside your product solution.

Another thing to keep in mind is that if building a product is like painting a mural, customers typically care about very specific areas of the mural. They'll tell you "I want this little section right here to be red. And that section over there...it really needs to be green for my needs." If you go off and build exactly what each customer asks for, it's like painting that mural with a paintball gun. A little splatter of paint here, and a little splatter of paint there. You won't build a coherent picture and you'll make a big mess.

Customers also expect magic. Be ready for that. Your product should just work for them. That's well within their rights. It's your job to listen to their magic needs and turn them into reality. That's what real magicians actually do. They think up something impossible (move this coin from one hand to another, make the Statue of Liberty disappear, cut that woman in half) and then think through the steps to make that impossibility a reality.
That's your job. You make magic happen.

A/B Testing

5 Seconds- Make a change and see if it's more popular than the status quo. Then iterate.

I have to admit, I'm no expert on A/B Testing. You'll find better sources elsewhere, but for some sense of completeness, I'm including this section here since this is what I wish I knew about A/B Testing when I started out as a product manager.

A/B Testing is a process by which you take your existing product and make a change to it. You let a subset of your customers see the change and then measure their reaction to it. If the reaction is good, you roll out the change to a larger group. If the reaction is bad, you revert the change.

You'll need some understanding of statistics to use A/B Testing. You can find some good courses on A/B Testing online at the following places: Udacity, Udemy, Coursera and I'm sure plenty of other places. The math isn't too difficult. Understanding what makes a good A/B Test isn't so straightforward though.

A couple things to know about A/B Testing. It's primarily for incremental changes. Want to find out if changing the color of the "Buy Now" button changes your conversion rate? Perfect for A/B Testing. Want to rebrand your product and overhaul your webpage? Not so great for A/B Testing. Second, the bigger the effect you expect, the smaller the sample size you need. Here's what I mean. You have two experiments: 1) you think changing the text on the call-to-action will increase conversion from 10% to 50% and 2) changing the color of the "Buy Now" button will increase conversion from 10% to 10.5%. Which of these two experiments will need more data? Surprisingly, the second one.

One challenge of A/B Testing is that it points you towards local optimizations.

Finally, A/B Testing doesn't tell you what you need to do next, but it can be wonderful validation of product improvements.

Section V: Prioritization & Backlog Management

5 Seconds- Knowing what needs to be done next is second only to knowing where you need to ultimately go. A good PM knows the most important thing for his team to work on.

One of your main jobs as a product manager is to prioritize the work for your engineering team. They will look to you to tell them the next thing to work on. Whether it's something as specific as backlog grooming so they know the next defects to work on or a bigger initiative like 'customer retention is more important than customer acquisition'.

Think of your engineering team as a beast that needs to be fed. Your job is to have their food ready to go and in bite sized chunks. An engineering team that's run out of food is a dangerous creature. But if you're trying to force feed your team with too many things at once, you're going to have problems.

You'll end up spending a good amount of your time thinking about and validating your assumptions to justify why *this* bit of work is more important than *that* bit of work.

The 'Why' is more important than the 'What'

5 Seconds- You need a framework in order to weigh your priorities. When you figure out *why* you want to do something, the *what* falls in line.

You're going to have a backlog of features and capabilities that you want your team to build. Your stakeholders will have their list of features and capabilities they want you to build. Your job is to convince your stakeholders that *your* prioritized list is the right list. Well, first, your job is to make sure that your list *is* the right list, *then* to convince others that it's right.

When I first started this, I'd get all the input. I'd figure out what I thought needed to happen next. In the spirit of compromise, I did my best to make sure everyone was equally unhappy. I kid, but honestly, if one department is too happy with your plan, chances are the other departments are super *unhappy* with it. So then I'd socialize the plan. "Here's what we're working on for the next few months."

And then I'd get hit with "why isn't *this* on the plan?" and "what about *that* thing that our big customer is screaming for?" And I'd have to justify my plan piecemeal. I'd find myself in negotiations with stakeholders. They'd want to horse-trade asking for *this* instead of *that*.

The best way to avoid this altogether is to craft your *why* before your *what*. I'm beginning to think I should have titled this book *Start With Why*, but a much more talented author has already taken that name.

What are the business drivers you're aiming for? What is the thematic focus of the next three to six months? Those decisions frame why you're doing the work. The work is in service of those business drivers. That's why you're doing what you're doing.

Now you'll have an answer to why *this* particular thing that I want isn't on the plan. Because it doesn't get us closer to our thematic objectives. Now the person objecting needs to make a case that your thematic objective isn't as important as what they want. You've raised the stakes for them. You've shifted the conversation to a more meaningful place while simultaneously staking out your territory ahead of time. You've thought this through. You've surveyed the landscape. You've framed the discussion and that's half the battle.

Just to be clear, I realize I'm using a battle analogy which may seem combative & short sighted. In reality, everyone in your company is on the same team. Your goal isn't to win or to defeat them. But your goal is to convince them and in order to do that, you may need to change their minds.

Buy a Feature

5 Seconds- Arbitrary constraints are a beautiful way to distill people's top priorities. And it's fun to watch them squirm.

So you've got a bunch of input on what your product needs. You have your own ideas. Customers have sent in requests. PreSales, Sales, Support, and the CEO all have their own thoughts on the topic. How can you get an accurate understanding of what people *really* want?

By making them pay for it.

This is a fun little game called Buy a Feature. With it, you can force your stakeholders to rank their requests in order of importance. If you just ask them "Which of these is not important", you'll get blank stares and a fight. Everything is important. If you give them fake money and say "Which of these will you buy right now" you'll get squirming & frustration, but they'll eventually put their money where their mouth is.

So how's it work?

Get a spreadsheet. Take your top 20-50 features you'd like to deliver and put them in a column. Price each one according to size. We use t-shirt sizing (i.e. S, M, L, XL). So a S would be $10, M: $30, L: $50, XL: $100. Invite your stakeholders to a meeting and give each of them their own column on the spreadsheet. Now give them some fake money. How much money? Tally up how much *everything* combined would cost to buy. Now divide that by 3 (or 4 if you want to be extra cruel) and this is how much money you're going to split amongst your stakeholders.

Example:
- I have 50 features I'm considering

- The total fake-dollar value of these feature is $1500
- Divide $1500 by 3 to get $500 to distribute amongst all the participants
- If 20 people show up, they each get $25*
- They now are free to put their $25 towards any feature they wish
- Tally up where people put their money
- Likely only 10-15% of the features will have been 'purchased'. These are what your participants feel is most valuable.

There's two big points I want to make right here: 1) a purchased feature does not commit me to building that feature next. I make this abundantly clear ahead of time. These Buy a Feature sessions are aids to help with prioritization and input. They are not a way for me to hand over the responsibility of the prioritization of work. 2) The conversation that happens during these sessions is often more valuable than the numbers on the spreadsheet. Participants will quickly realize they need to team up in order to afford just about anything. You get to hear them argue their case for this instead of that to get others on board. Listen closely to these conversations. They're invaluable. Also, if someone puts money towards a feature you didn't expect, ask them why. That's what you're digging for. The why. What is it about this that is so critical? Keep pulling the thread.

I'll say it again, it's so important to have these Buy a Feature sessions live. I used to get pushback on this. "If the information is on a Google spreadsheet, why can't I just fill it out whenever?". It's because I want to be a fly on the wall when you get frustrated that the thing that will make your life better isn't getting voted on. I want to hear you fight for it. I want to hear you argue and convince others that it's in their best interest to prioritize what you want.

Why does Buy a Feature work?

Because you're forcing people to work within constraints. Left to their own devices, they'd be a kid in a candy store. Just asking for anything & everything. Now they have to really think about what's most important to them.

It helps set expectations. When stakeholders see a feature go unpurchased, they realize that it's likely not going to be prioritized for some period of time. You've just helped set feature delivery expectations for a wide swath of your organization.

I've said it before, but it merits saying again: a Buy a Feature session does not obligate you to do *anything*. The roadmap is still yours to set. Buy a Feature sessions are simply a tool you can use to help you prioritize. I highly recommend trying them out.

* How you split the money is up to you. You can be perfectly democratic and split evenly or you can give some people more than others based on whatever criteria you decide.

Frameworks

5 Seconds- It's easier to make a lot of small decisions than one or two big ones. Prioritization frameworks help you make those smaller decisions and give a sense of objectivity to your roadmap.

So you've got your backlog of features you know you need to build. You've got feedback from internal and external stakeholders. You have your *why*. Now it's time to come up with the *what*. You need a ranked order of priorities to funnel to your engineering team. This doesn't need to be a massive list. This needs to be enough to give your team a sense of direction and enough so that you don't starve their pipeline of work.

What to do?

One option is to sit and ponder your choices. Literally get a list and start moving stuff around. *This* will be the #1 thing we do next. Then *that* one. This something else is third. If you're lucky and I mean really lucky, you may have a good sense of the top 3-4 things. After that, it gets incredibly tricky. Is this one 11th or 12th? How can you be sure? It's like college football. It's typically not hard to pick the top 2-3 teams in order, but what really separates #8 from #9? Or #15 from #16?

This is why you need a framework that spits out a number for each feature you care about.

Luckily, you have options. Your company may have already adopted one of these. If so, stick with it. Remember, you're not out to change your company yet. Even if you don't think it's the best framework, stick with it. Learn it and understand its strengths & weaknesses.

Here's some prioritization frameworks in no particular order.

- RICE- Reach, Impact, Confidence, Effort

- MoSCoW method- https://en.wikipedia.org/wiki/MoSCoW_method
- Kano method
- Weighted Shortest Job First- https://www.scaledagileframework.com/wsjf/

Each of these methods attempts to break down the *why* of each feature into component parts. Then they will spit out a somewhat objective ranking for your features to help you make a more calculated, objective decision around what to do next.

Backlogs- what are they?

5 Seconds- Your backlog is either a ranked list of 'next-up work' or it's a storage shed that you never clean out. I propose you have one of each.

The fastest way to get someone to stop harassing you for a feature is to finally cave in and say "ok, it's on the backlog". They'll get the impression that you have it in some queue getting ready to be worked on when in reality, you've taken their request and tossed it into that old storage shed out back. You've successfully told the truth and completely failed to set expectations. Now in a couple months, that same person will come back and won't be distracted by the fancy "backlog" excuse. They'll ask when their feature is getting built. For this, you won't have a good answer.

Your backlog is work you want to get done that you're not actively working on right now. That's it. The confusing part is there's a couple different sizes of work. And when people talk about something being on the backlog, they rarely discuss it in terms of the size of the work and more importantly, which type of backlog they're referring to. This leads to mismatched expectations which is the bane of product managers everywhere.

Backlog 1

This is the smallest backlog with the smallest sized chunks of work. This is the task and story level work that engineers take on during standups.

In teams doing scrum with two week sprints, this backlog should be small enough that the team can reasonably be expected to finish it in a couple sprints. As work gets completed and the backlog shrinks, you can add more stories, tasks and defects to the backlog to keep it at a reasonable size. In other words, be a minimalist with this backlog. The tendency will be to continue adding defects and nice-to-have stories to this backlog in hopes of getting to them 'someday'. Believe me when I say that someday will never come. And when it does come, something else will be more pressing. Be ruthless in closing out minor defects. If they're not important enough to do with the next month, they're not important enough to do. Those nice-to-haves will clutter your backlog and generate mental strain every time you have to pass over them to prioritize the must-haves. Be ruthless here. Be a minimalist.

Mary Poppendieck makes a good case why this backlog should be reduced to the bare minimum: https://thenewstack.io/mary-poppendieck-on-why-you-should-just-burn-your-backlog/

Backlog 2

This one is for bigger work. You can think of this as all the features you know you're going to want to put in your product.

I have less actionable advice here. I want to say 'be a minimalist' and keep this down to the work you think you'll get to over the next 6 months. I've not been good about this. I've been a hoarder for this larger backlog. It's not ideal, but when you're brainstorming all the things you know you'll need to build, you want to keep that list somewhere. You don't want to go through a multi-day product strategy session with post-its everywhere and all the different great stuff to build, only to throw away 90% of it because you only want to focus on the here and now.

In theory, I want to say be a minimalist here also, but in reality, I can't say that I've followed my own advice.

Hoarder or Minimalist

5 Seconds- Decide early if you want to keep everything (i.e. be a hoarder) or only keep the very most critical work (i.e. be a minimalist). Trying to walk a middle ground will get you run over.

See the previous essay.

Do your best to decide whether you're going to collect everything or whether you're going to watch your backlog like a hawk. One takes effort up front, the other takes additional mental overhead when you're prioritizing. One requires a lot of difficult, often unnecessary conversations where you have to tell people "no" straight out. You have to say "I realize this is a reasonable feature request, but I'm not going to put it on my backlog. I'm not going to record it. It's simply not getting done." While a principled approach, that kind of conversation won't make you any friends.

On the other hand, keeping everything means you don't have those confrontational conversations, but it may be difficult to find anything. Or more likely, you'll have a somewhat ordered list of 'next up' features, and then an unordered mess beneath that. You may find that you'll create a feature in your backlog only to realize weeks later that you *already* had that feature in your backlog, so now you've got duplicates.

What about the middle way? The Goldilocks path? Not too much, not too little, but *juuust* right? It's an ideal worth pursuing and if you ever get there, let me know how you do it.

Communicate, Communicate, Communicate

5 Seconds- If you don't tell people your plans, prepare to have them changed.

So you've done all the right things. You've reached out to customers for input. You've met with internal stakeholders to see what their needs are. You've run all your features through a prioritization framework. You understand the market needs and how you're going to solve them. You now have a roadmap of well ordered features and capabilities. You know what your product will look like in 3 months, 9 months, 18 months. Let's assume you've magically done all this. Now what?

You have to tell people. You have to become the Chief Marketing Officer for your roadmap. You have to announce this to the world (and by world, I mean everyone in your company). Don't be shy. Your first inclination may be to hold your plans close to your chest. You're thinking "this is my baby. This roadmap is mine...all mine." You want to protect it from people who just don't understand. Resist that urge. Don't be Gollum, hiding in a cave hunched over repeating "My precious".

Socialize your plans. Remember all those stakeholders. The flow of communication isn't one way from them to you. You owe it to them to prepare them for what's coming next.

I'll expand on this in a later section and go into more depth on what each stakeholder group wants and needs to hear, but for now, let's talk about two primary reasons for this communication:

First and foremost, you want to prepare stakeholders for what's coming. Outside of Christmas morning, no one likes surprises. Even if you're building all the right things, different parts of your organization need to be ready for the new product capabilities. Engineering needs to be ready to build it. Marketing needs to know how to position it. Sales needs to know how to sell it. The CEO and Chief Product Officer need to buy into the vision of the product and where you're taking it. This is a nicer way of saying, you need to ensure that the direction you want to take the product is aligned with the CPO & CEO. More delicately, you may want to socialize your roadmap with customers. I'll get into this more later, but customers buy based on what you have today, but they also buy based on your vision and future capabilities. It's a dance since you don't want to over-promise and set impossible expectations, but giving them some insight into the future can be a good thing.

Second, you want to give people a chance to tell you you're wrong early. Trust me, it's better to find out your plan isn't perfect early. If you protect your roadmap & prioritized features from scrutiny, you won't get that feedback. I have a strong belief that all of us is smarter than any of us. Pardon the poor english, but you get the meaning. I'd rather be told I'm wrong early than to build the wrong thing. Your roadmap is antifragile. Antifragile is a term I learned from Nassim Nicholas Talib. "Some things benefit from shocks; they thrive and grow when exposed to volatility…The resilient resists shocks and stays the same; the antifragile gets better"

I'll talk more later about all the places you should communicate your plans. For now, here's a short list:

- On-demand
    - Put it in a wiki or give people read-only access to your prioritization tool
- Scheduled presentations
    - Give presentations monthly or quarterly to various stakeholders
    - Invite feedback

If your plans are locked away in a vault that no one else has access to, you're doing it wrong.

Section VI: Working With Engineers

5 Seconds- Engineers are a special breed. If you know how to work with them, they can move mountains. If you don't know how to work with them, they'll make you look stupid...which you are, because you couldn't work with the people who build your product.

Engineers are often either lionized or demonized. They're either supernatural beings that use the dark arts of coding to perform magic, or they're temperamental, fussy prima donnas who force you to kowtow to them to get them to do anything for you. Both these sentiments are wrong.

A good engineering team can make you look like a genius, but in reality, you're responsible for helping your team make you look good. Engineers are people. They want to do good work, but they have very different needs than you do. Understanding those needs and acting accordingly is your responsibility.

You are a hummingbird. Engineers are elephants.

5 Seconds- Different animals experience time differently. Product Managers and Engineers are different animals. Time flows differently for these two roles.

I had to learn this one the hard way. Part of why I'm writing this is so that you don't have to.

I read an article by Isaac Asimov once where he did some back of the envelope math and figured out that most animals have a maximum life expectancy of about 1 billion heartbeats. There's even a research project to collect data on this (http://robdunnlab.com/projects/beats-per-life/). As an aside, humans are huge outliers on this spectrum. We get over twice this number of heartbeats, but that's due to indoor plumbing and antibiotics, but I digress.

What's this mean on a practical level? It means that if you take a video of an elephant and speed it up so that the heart rate of the elephant in the video is equivalent to the heart rate of say a mouse, the pack of elephants will scurry around on screen and look so very similar to a pack of mice flitting here and there dashing and eating. Different animals have different internal clocks.

Remember this when working with engineers. You're like a hummingbird. You're flying back and forth between stakeholder meetings, planning sessions, customer calls, status meetings with management, oh, and standups with engineers. Engineers are like elephants. They're slowly moving big heavy loads. They look like they're plodding away. You're flying around wondering what's taking them so long.

When I say "slow", it only looks slow to you. Engineers are spending time doing deep thinking. They're working on a complex problem and trying to think about all the implications and how it's going to work given the constraints of the current code. It takes them time to load all this information into their heads. It's not easy.

Then, you get hit with a customer fire. You fly over to your pack of elephants and chirp: "Drop everything! We need to fix this *now*!" It takes time for the pack to set down their load. It takes time to reorient to the problem at hand. They have to pick up this new problem. Your heart rate is at 600 bpm. Theirs is at 30 bpm. They're moving as fast as they know how and yet they're moving at 1/20th of what you *think* they should be. Unless you appreciate the different perspectives of time, you'll cause whiplash, burnout & resentment.

You wonder why they aren't able to react as fast as you. But then you realize that one elephant can move more than a thousand hummingbirds. Both roles are needed. Without the elephants, nothing would ever get moved. Without the hummingbirds, you'd have an elephant coordinating the work.

This isn't to suggest you never redirect or that you shield them from every interrupt. It's only to show that interruptions & redirections have a cost and that you are careful and deliberate when introducing them.

Get tight with your engineering manager

5 Seconds- Your engineering manager is the most important person in the company. A good working relationship with that person is worth its weight in gold.

Your engineering manager isn't objectively *the* most important person in the company, but from your perspective you should treat them if they were.

Typically you'll be attached to a team of 5-10 engineers who all report to a single engineering manager. This person has an engineering background and decided at some point to move into a management career path instead of an individual contributor career path. One path isn't better than the other, but the responsibilities are quite different. Anyway, the engineering manager is in charge of HR issues, approving vacation, counseling, professional development of the engineers, etc. They also have 'been there, done that' so not only do the engineers on your team have to give them deference because of the position, they also give deference because the engineering manager has typically seen these problems before and can give advice & guidance.

Get tight with your engineering manager. When you need something done, go to the engineering manager. Don't go straight to your favorite engineer. The engineering manager should have the pulse of the team. They will know what each person is working on and will be able to direct your request to the right person. They can act as a senior advisor to you and can tell you if you're trying to implement anti-patterns and will also act as a traffic cop to direct the right work to the right people.

Ask them what they've seen that works. You're likely not the first product manager they've worked with. Although they don't know how to do your job, they've seen other people do it enough to tell you if you're screwing up with the team.

Engineering Managers are closer to hummingbirds than they are to elephants. They used to be an elephant and understand the behaviors and needs of the engineers, but since they've moved into management, their days are filled with more meetings and impromptu calls than they used to be. You should be touching base with your engineering manager daily if not more often.

Make friends with your engineering manager. Get their advice. Funnel work through them. You'll be happier. Engineers will be happier. You'll have a better team.

Bring problems, not solutions

5 Seconds- Problems promote creativity & new ideas. Solutions treat people like automatons without free will. Engineers like problems. You like problems.

This is a common pattern I used to find myself in. A customer or another internal stakeholder would come to me. "We need *this* to change. And here's how to change it." I'd listen to them, write down what they said and then take that to engineering. "Hey engineers, we need *this* to change and here's how to change it."

Engineering would then ask "but what's the problem"

Me: The problem is that *this* hasn't been changed yet. I've told you what you need to know. Here's how to change it.

Engineering: But what's the problem you're trying to solve?

Me: The problem was that we didn't have this feature. Now the problem is that you're not listening to me.

We'd go back and forth like this. I thought I was being helpful by bringing them a solution. "Make this change", but the engineers I worked with rightly understood that I didn't fully appreciate the problem. There could be other solutions that not only would solve the problem at hand, but also other problems I'd not even considered.

I was also taking the autonomy of the engineers. They're not translators who take english and turn it into code. They're problem solvers. They're creatives. I was cutting them off at the knee.

As you progress, you'll see this pattern with customers. They'll bring you solutions and you'll have to push back to get to the root of the problem.

Use the 5-why's approach. Keep digging and ask why. When you get that answer, ask why *that* is important. I learned about the 5-why's approach when I was in the Navy. We used it for root-cause analysis. The ultimate cause of the problem isn't the surface symptom. It's always something deeper. You want to get deep into the root of the problem, only then can you work on what can be done to fix it..

Treat your engineers how you want customers to treat you. Let them flex their creative muscles. You'll be amazed what they can do.

What are the types of work?

5 Seconds- There's different types of deliverables engineers can work on. Feature work is just one aspect. Defects, Technical Debt, and Risk are other important things you need to consider.

Most of the time in Product Management interviews, you'll be asked to design a feature. You'll be asked how to prioritize features. You'll be asked how you know if a feature is successful or not. You may begin to think that the only type of work you need to concern yourself with is Features. Be careful of that assumption.

Engineers on your team have a variety of tasks and commitments that will rightfully take them away from direct Feature work. Let's explore some of these areas now.

Features are the easiest to explain. Features are net new functionality in your product that benefit the customer. Customers are able to do something they previously couldn't do. The definition of 'customer' may get a bit hazy. Paying customers are definitely customers. What about internal stakeholders? Is your support team a customer? I'd argue that they are. What if you're on a platform team that delivers functionality to a customer-facing product team. Is that team a customer? I'd say they are. I don't want to get too much into the weeds here though. The take home message is that a feature gives customers more good stuff.

Next comes Defects. While it may seem like it's easy to define a defect, you'll often find yourself arguing "This isn't a defect. The product is working as designed. You're asking for a new feature". Here's my definition: a defect is anytime the product isn't working as advertised. When I say "as advertised", I mean that the product doesn't do something that your company claims it does. If you've got bad documentation, you're going to have defects because the customer can point to section x.x and say "you told me it can do *this*, but it doesn't". Other times, if the product itself claims to do something, but can't, that's a defect. If there's a "download here" button, but nothing downloads, then regardless of your documentation, you've got a defect. Part of your team's time is going to be fixing defects. You need to account for that in your planning. So defects provide your customers with 'less bad' stuff.

Next up is Technical Debt. Personally I loath the term 'technical debt'. I like to think of this as 'technical investment', but if you read about this, you'll always hear it referred to as debt. Don't worry, we're talking about the same thing. Your engineers will understand this one and there's plenty of books and articles about it. Technical Debt (or investment) is work your team will do so that they can work faster and more efficiently in the future. Your company benefits because your team is able to work more efficiently in the future. You're investing in your future by paying down old debt. This type of work spans the gamut, from building an automated testing suite, to replacing an outdated front-end framework, to massive backend refactoring (i.e. cleaning up confusing code). If you're not spending some of your time investing in the future, you'll find yourself unable to move fast. If you're chopping trees, sharpening your axe is technical debt. Working on technical debt directly benefits your team since it allows for better working conditions. So debt work provides *you* with more good.

The last big flavor of work is Risk work. This one is a bit more nebulous. The other three can be broken down as follows: Does it give the customer more good? If so, it's a feature. Does it give the customer less bad? Then it's a feature. Does it give you, the vendor, more good? Then it's Technical Debt (or as I like to call it, Technical Investment). So there's one category we've left off: Does it give you, the vendor, less bad?

What does this mean 'less bad'? Risk work is the effort you spend to protect yourself from something that may never happen, but if it did, could be catastrophic. It's an expense. Improving your password encryption technology is Risk work. Customers only indirectly benefit and it's not going to help you move faster in the future, in fact some Risk work will actually slow you down. I like to think of Risk work as hiring a security guard. They reduce the risk of burglary, but don't prevent it altogether. It's hard to determine the ROI because the return is based on the unknown of what didn't happen. Loss prevention won't pay the bills like new shiny features, but failing to invest in loss prevention can result in your company going under if something bad does happen.

This list isn't all inclusive. There's investigatory work. There's questions from support that require engineering expertise. There's documentation. The list goes on. That said, if you're not thinking about the big four types of work above, you're planning for disaster. You're upsetting new & existing customers (failure to do feature work). You're losing existing customers (not fixing defects). Your ability to deliver new value is slowly grinding to a halt (failure to work on technical debt). Or you're leaving the door open to security risks and raising the possibility of being sued or breached by bad actors (failure to invest in risk work).

You, or someone in your company, should be thinking about the distribution of your work. Where are you investing your team's time? Understanding the different areas of investment is a good first step.

Engineers are optimists. Don't believe them.

5 Seconds- Engineers do not want to disappoint, so they give optimistic estimates. Be careful about socializing those timelines.

If you remember nothing else, remember Hofstadler's Law which states "It always takes longer than you expect, even when you take into account **Hofstadter's Law**". The recursive nature of the sentence is intentional.

You may not have heard of Douglas Hofstadter, but you may have heard of *Godel, Escher, Bach*. It won the Pulitzer, but beware, it's a monster of a book, and while brilliant is very complex. *I am a Strange Loop* is a bit more accessible and I'd recommend reading it first since mere mortals stand a chance of understanding it.

Anyway, the point here is that even when an engineer gives you their best estimate, they're likely forgetting to take something into account. I recently had an engineer give an estimate that something would be done in two weeks. That sounded fine, except that it was already Tuesday, we had a day of engineering meetings on Thursday and he was slated to take the on-call rotation the following week and we knew that the on-call week was never very productive. When I pointed this out to him, he revised his estimate to be 3-4 weeks out. When he heard "how long", he immediately went to "how long will it take assuming I'm not distracted and am able to focus *just* on this thing".

This is also your fault. Engineers have seen your type before. They give an estimate. You don't like it. You push on them. They have a couple choices. They stick to their guns and you continue the conflict. Or option two, they try to make everyone happy and revise their estimate to something shorter. With option two, you're happy.

For now. So engineers have been trained to just give in. It's not good. It's not ideal. But it's reality.

So you get an estimate. Don't wait until the day before the estimated completion date to get a revised update. I remember in little-league soccer practice, the coaches would make us run sprints from the goal posts to the coach. Then the coach would start running backwards. That's what finishing a feature is often like. The initial estimate is the distance from the goal to the coach, but the finish line keeps getting further away.

Why do I say this? Two reasons. First, so you're not surprised when it takes longer than you expect (even when you take into account Hofstadter's Law. Second, since such a big part of your job is expectation setting, you need to know how to set those expectations. You'll be on the other side of this pressure when you present plans to your boss or to your sales team. They'll want the work faster. They'll push back on your estimate. You'll have to decide whether you want to disappoint them now...or later.

Trust me. It's better to have the confrontation now.

Engineering Career Paths

5 Seconds- Engineers typically take one of two paths: 1) individual contributor or 2) management. Understanding these paths & why someone would choose one over the other will help your relationships.

As a Product Manager, you're not going to be responsible for the career progression of the engineering you work with. Engineering career coaching is the responsibility of their Engineering Manager. Even though it's not your responsibility, I find it's useful to understand the career goals of the people around you.

Most engineers want to become great individual contributors. They want to build great code themselves and to influence their team to be better. They want to work on hard problems and solve them. Most engineers want to be stronger elephants. They want to move heavy things. You need these folks in your company and on your team.

There are a few engineers you'll run across that will migrate towards the managerial route. You won't find any great correlation between engineering acumen and managerial acumen, so don't assume that only your best engineers will want to become managers. Just as the greatest athletes don't become the best coaches. These folks will be the ones who want to take on the additional extra-curricular activities of organizing meetings and facilitating meetings. They're the ones who you see translating engineering-speak into product-speak and business-speak when your team is having deep technical and architectural conversations. They're the ones you turn to when you need understanding.

As a PM, you should look for these characteristics and give feedback to the engineering managers. Neither of these career tracks is better or worse than the other. Both are needed. There is a different skill set required to move into management and it's not just a continuation of typical engineering skills, it requires a bit of a pivot for the engineer.

Section VII: Roadmaps and Release Plans

5 Seconds- You need to be able to advertise what's coming in the product. Understanding the purpose of roadmaps and release plans will help you make them better.

A large part of your job as a product manager is to set expectations. Your team needs to know what work is coming. Your sales and marketing departments need to know what new capabilities they'll be able to talk about. You get the idea.

Roadmaps & Release Plans are one mechanism to help you set expectations. They have different purposes and time horizons, but ultimately, they're wonderful communication tools if used correctly.

Roadmaps vs. Release Plans: What are they?

5 Seconds- Stakeholders need to know where your product is going. Roadmaps and release plans are similar, but different ways to tell them.

In the world of product management, you need to have a vision of where your product is going. Where will it evolve? Your stakeholders need to understand this also. Roadmaps and release plans are your tools of communication. In my experience, roadmaps and release plans have different time horizons.

Roadmaps are directionally correct, aspirational presentations. Many things will change between the time you present a roadmap and the time you actualize it. Customers want to see that you have a long-term vision. They want to know that the product they're investing in will grow over the coming years.

Release plans are shorter-term presentations. They describe the near-term commitments you plan to build. Release plans are more concrete than Roadmaps.

In my experience, release plans are more internally focused, and roadmaps are more externally focused.

Your company may have different names for roadmaps and release plans and if they do, go with that terminology, but I suspect the goals of the different presentations will match closely to these terms.

Why two types of presentations?

5 Seconds- Roadmaps & release plans have different time horizons and different goals. One is to educate, the other is to sell.

When looking into the future, it's important to have different focal points.

There's a long-term, aspirational, anything-goes focal point. I like to frame this in terms of what could the product look like five years from now? Your product is going to change the world in 5 years. It's going to be bigger than you can imagine. Don't hold back when thinking about the 5-year vision.

There's the closer in 1-year time horizon. This is what I like to call the adjacent-possible. You can't get here today, but it's where you want to see the product when you look up from the immediate needs of your customers and stakeholders. Although there are hurdles to reaching this vision, you can see and identify almost all of the hurdles. In the 5 year vision, you barely see glimpses of the longer-term hurdles.

Then there's the 1-3 month time horizon. This comprises the immediate concrete work you know you need to do. You've discussed this work with engineering. You likely have wireframes and requirements set.

Roadmaps draw heavily on the 1-year vision and borrow a bit on the short-term vision and a bit on the long-term aspirations. Roadmaps are generally externally facing. They're meant to sell the vision of the product. Your goal is to give a bit of concreteness to prove that your product is evolving in tangible ways, but it's also to keep the spectators interested in the future.

Release plans are focused on immediate, near-term needs. I find these to be more internally facing and show more of the ugly underbelly of the product. I'm more likely to talk about embarrassing technical debt that needs to be dealt with in a Release Plan. I want to explain why engineering isn't 100% focused on new features for the sales team. Some of the technical debt work and risk work isn't something I typically socialize with customers.

"But we're agile" I hear you saying, "what's up with having a release plan? Why would you lock yourself into a 3-month plan?" Good question. We're agile also and always caveat our release plans by saying plans can change if circumstances require it. The release plan is just that, a plan. It's not a commitment. It's what we'd do today if we didn't learn anything new. Presenting in this way every quarter to the rest of the company keeps everyone informed of our intentions and general direction.

This is why I like to keep these two types of presentations separate in my mind. Each depends on the audience and why you're presenting to them. It can be that you present a roadmap to internal stakeholders, but then the goal of that presentation is not to arm them for what's coming in the next 3 months. It's to inspire them and help them see the long-term vision of the product. You can present a release plan to a customer, but if you do, they may only care about one or two things that immediately affect them.

Their Flexible Nature

5 Seconds- Plans are nothing; planning is everything. - Eisenhower

Plans change. Get over it. When presented with new information, you need to adapt. Even after weeks of planning & prioritization to craft the perfect short-term release plan, you may be presented with new information that throws your plan out the window.

That's to be expected.

It's not the plan that's important. It's your planning process. It's the *why* behind your prioritization.

If you know your why then you'll know how to incorporate the new information. How does this information jibe with the product strategy? Is it in line with fulfilling the strategy? Great! Then you have the opportunity to do more to fulfill your strategy. Is this new information counter to your strategy? Great! Then you have a great argument why you shouldn't be distracted by this news.

Here's an example. Your strategy is to focus on renewals. Everyone agrees. Your release plan is 100% focused on features to generate renewals. Now, your sales team has just told you that they can open up a huge new pipeline of customers if only you build some net new feature to attract that new customer base. What do you do? Based on the stated strategy, you've got to tell the sales team "sorry, but not now". Renewals are more important than net new customers. But what if your strategy had been "Grow the customer base by 30%"? In that case, you may have been given a gift on a silver platter. Your plans *should* change in light of this opportunity to get a whole new batch of customers.

In this example, you must ensure that your product strategy is aligned with the business strategy. That's often harder than you may think.

Be proud of your roadmap, but not so proud that you can't kill it and start over if and when the world changes beneath your feet.

Sell your vision

5 Seconds- Roadmaps and release plans are your chance to convince stakeholders you know what you're doing.

A common misconception about roadmaps and release plans is that they're to educate customers and stakeholders about what you plan to build. That's a short-term, myopic view of the world. I had this misconception for longer than I care to admit.

The 'what are we building' view focuses on the "what". What's coming next? What are we doing? And by omission, what are we not doing?

You're missing a huge opportunity to sell your vision if you work this way.

Roadmaps and release plans are your opportunity to sell the *why*. You get to set the stage and educate your audience on the important drivers of your product and the business in general.

Is the focus on net new customers? Is it converting & upselling existing customers? Is it operational maturity? Is it cost reduction? What are the criteria by which you judged the various features in your backlog? Start there. Start with the why and only then go into the what.

This does a few things for you. First, you're framing the discussion. Disagreements are typically won by the person who is able to frame their arguments better. Once you define the playing field, you're likely to come out ahead. Second, it gives the audience confidence in the how of your prioritization. They'll care less about the specific things you're building, but they'll walk away with a sense of the themes you're working towards.

Focusing on why gets you closer to the 'who cares' part of the roadmap or release plan. It's so easy to get caught up in the details that you forget to sell the benefits of what you're doing.

Gaining leadership's confidence is a key step in your product management journey. Getting to the why behind your roadmaps is a great way to build that confidence.

Section VIII: Working With Sales

5 Seconds- Salespeople are a unique bunch. If you understand them, they'll make you look great. Without them, your product may fail.

Salespeople are unique animals. I tried my hand at sales and failed. Sales folks can get a bad rap. They can be pushy. You may think they're trying to coerce you to buy something you don't want.

Good salespeople are amazing. You need to understand they have a different skill set than you and have different incentives.

Sales is Coin-operated

5 Seconds- Salespeople are incentivized to sell. They follow the money.

Your sales team can be the most frustrating group of people you work with. They don't listen. They don't understand the product. They're always asking for stuff that's outside your vision.

What are they good for?

They're good for selling your product. Sure, sometimes you're going to be lucky enough to work at a company where the product sells itself. Assume that won't be you (even though you should always be pushing for product-led growth). You're going to rely on sales folks to put the product in one hand of the customer and to take money from the other hand.

Sales folks are coin-operated. Put in a coin, get out a result. This may sound dismissive, but I have the utmost respect for good salespeople. They have a risky job. If they don't meet their numbers, they get fired. If you release a bad feature, you say "fail fast" and release another feature. If salespeople fail fast, they lose their jobs.

Sales follow the incentive structure. Where do they think they can make the most money? Is it selling your product or another product?

When you appreciate the 'coin-operated' nature of Sales, many other things become more clear.

Sales Can't Wait for the Vision

5 Seconds- Sales cares about what you have *now*. You want it that way.

You've spent hours and days putting together a presentation to showcase the vision of your product. You're happy & proud. You present it to Sales and a month later, your sales have plummeted. Why?

Because Sales needs to sell what's on the truck today. Your job is to load up the truck with amazing stuff and educate Sales about the benefits you're providing to the customer. The sales team's job is to sell what's on the truck. Your vision presentation just confused them. You just talked about amazing capabilities and benefits that won't be available for months if not years.

You just discounted the value of what's on the truck. Sales stopped being excited about selling what you have today. They're now excited about what you're going to build tomorrow. The problem is that they can't sell it today. So they go one of two ways: 1) they wait, or 2) they sell on a promise. If they wait, then your numbers go down. Sales stops pushing the current product and they decide to wait until next year. In the meantime, they go off and sell some other product. Or, instead, they sell on a promise. They make a deal on the guarantee that some feature or capability will be there for this customer. That puts you in a bad spot since you're now going to have an angry customer with a legal contract in their hands.

I'm not saying that you should never, ever, ever let Sales know what you've got coming, but you should be very, very, very careful when you do present this to them. Make sure you've framed it appropriately. Make sure you put in plenty of caveats. Make sure your head of sales is on board and that you have a good relationship so they can head off any potential painful promises to customers.

Most importantly, never give off the impression that what you have *today* is anything less than amazing.

Inspire Confidence in the Product

5 Seconds- If your sales team doesn't have confidence that your product works, they'll stop selling it.

I realize I said that Sales is coin-operated and they follow the money. That's a bit short-sighted. Sales wants to keep making sales. They want to go back to your existing customers and upsell them or cross-sell.

If you convince your sales team that you have a better mousetrap, they'll walk into a meeting with their head held high with the confidence to tell the customer that your product will solve their problems.

Sales doesn't want to be blindsided by customer complaints due to a subpar product. If you give Sales a reason to doubt your product, you demotivate their desire to sell.

Be careful taking direction from your Sales team

5 Seconds- Your sales team will try to convince you that with *this one* feature, they can sell a huge new contract. Be wary of that promise.

Occasionally, you'll get customers who are perfectly happy with your product just the way it is. More often than not, especially if you're selling a B2B product, customers are going to have some big requests. If you have a sales team, they get stuck in the middle.

One one side is the customer with money in hand offering it up if only the product had this one particular feature. You're on the other side with an engineering team up to their neck in work and a backlog a mile long. And the sales rep is stuck in the middle.

The customer wants their feature. You want a robust product with capabilities inline with the product vision. The sales rep wants the commission. You're going to feel a great deal of pressure to make an exception for this customer. You'll hear that the quarterly sales goals are dependent on it. You'll hear that although this may be a small deal, there's a huge expansion upside and we just need to get our foot in the door. You'll feel stuck. On the one hand, you want to help the company make money on this particular customer, but on the other hand, you want a coherent product that's not a cobbled together Frankenstein's monster.

There's nothing wrong with reprioritizing a (previously) low priority feature to satisfy a customer. That ensures you're getting the most value out the door as quickly as possible. The challenge comes when the customer wants something outside the vision of the product or worse, a custom feature that only they will use.

If you're a junior PM, look to the more senior people in your organization for how to handle this. At my company, we have a designation to flag a request as a 'Deal Breaking Request'. The purpose was to raise the visibility of this to management. This escalation did two things: 1) prevented sales reps from making everything a deal-breaker and 2) let our Chief Product Officer weigh in. Regardless of whether we did or didn't decide to prioritize the request, we made sure everyone on the Management team understood the implications and trade-offs.

This was our process and it made sure that we kept the integrity of the product intact. Your company may have a different process. But the key takeaway is that you should definitely take input from your Sales organization, but if you let them set the vision & roadmap, your company will never get where it wants to go.

Section IX: Working With Customers

5 Seconds- Customers are the lifeblood of your product. Without them, you're dead in the water. That said, customers are distracted, finicky, and don't know what they want. It's your job to help them.

Without customers, you're nothing. You've got a hobby of building something. Without customers, you don't have a product. You don't have revenue. You're twisting in the wind.

With customers, you have a needy, cranky, distracted mob trying to pull you in 15 different directions and most of them are not in line with your vision. You're trying to build a car and they keep asking for a faster horse.

Let's be clear, I'm being intentionally overly dramatic. I'm pointing out the negatives since the positives are more self evident and easier to deal with. Customers can be fantastic advocates for you, your product and your company. Few things are better than a customer testimonial. But in this section, I'm focusing on the challenges I wish I knew when I started in this line of work.

They're running for dinner. You're running for your life.

5 Seconds- You are but one problem in your customer's day.

There's an old parable that resonates with me. One day, a fox saw a bunny rabbit in a field and thought "That looks like a tasty meal". He snuck up behind the rabbit and tried to catch it. As fast as he ran, the rabbit was quicker. The fox ran and ran, but the rabbit kept zigging and zagging. Eventually, the fox got tired and walked away with its tail between its legs. The foxes friend saw this whole thing go down and started making fun of the fox. "You couldn't catch that little rabbit! You must feel so embarrassed." The fox did feel a little embarrassed, but said "Yes, the rabbit got away, but you see, where I was running for dinner, the rabbit was running for his life."

The point is that the incentives for the rabbit and the fox were very different. A loss for one is an inconvenience. A loss for the other meant their life. I remind myself of this parable often. You're the bunny. Other people are foxes. They don't realize the effect they may have on you...and that's ok. The fox has no malice towards the bunny. It's hungry and wants to be satisfied. Once I came to terms with that, I realized I'm not really going to be eaten, even if it feels that way.

Customers are going to take out their frustration on you. They get that right when they pay you. Customers are going to ask for off-the-wall things. It's because those problems are the foxes that are chasing them. Everyone thinks of themselves as the rabbit.

Imagine this. You're running a beta program and need feedback. Getting the customer set up & running is the most important thing you have to do. For them, it's an inconvenience. You may prepare for hours for your call. They may skip it. It's not out of spite or any malicious intent. It's that you're just not as important to them as they are to you.

Remember, they're just running for dinner. They don't realize that you're running for your life.

Customers suck at explaining problems. They're great at providing solutions.

5 Seconds- Customers try to be helpful by giving you the answer to the problem they want solved. You need to keep pushing to figure out the problem.

We covered this in the section about working with engineers. Remember how you need to give them problems and not provide them with solutions? Your customers haven't read that part of this book.

When you first start working with customers, be very careful when they give you suggestions & recommendations. You'll think they're giving you a gift. You'll think they're removing the need for hard questions and investigation. You'll think "they just gave me the answer to a question I didn't know I had". You'll be wrong.

Couple things. First, you'll be short-changing yourself. You need to understand why that solution is useful. You need to dig into the problem they're trying to solve. It could be that their problem is shared by many, but their solution will only work for them. Now you've built a custom feature that won't scale to the reset of your user base.

Second, you're letting your creative muscle atrophy. Your job as a product manager is to look at problems and find creative solutions. Have you ever seen those art installations where it looks like a pile of trash from most angles, but if you stand in just the right spot, and have just the right perspective, all the random junk forms a face? Your job as a PM is to learn to find that perspective. Where all the random stuff 'fits'. It takes time and energy and experience to gain that perspective. Letting a customer dictate the solution is taking a shortcut.

You're not doing them any good and you're not doing yourself any good.

Taking the customer solution is taking the easy way out.

The right thing to do is to listen attentively while they tell you what you should build and to ask "but what is the problem you're having?"

They'll cock their head to one side and think you're crazy. "My problem is that I don't have <insert feature here>."

Keep going from different angles. Keep probing. It may turn out that they do, in fact, have the best idea, but that's the rare exception.

I read something once that said customers are 'always correct about quality, sometimes correct about exact problems, and never correct about solutions.' I try to keep that in mind.

Customers buy for what the product is today and for what it will be in the future

5 Seconds- People buy on the promise of a better future.

I don't know what the exact formula is, but I'm confident there's some combination of existing features and potential future features that actually determines the customer's buying potential.

I think the buying potential is related to the emotional connection to your product. How you feel about a product is some combination of how well that product has served you in the past, how well it's serving you today and what you think it can do for you in the future. That all that gets divided by the current pain of using the product today (i.e. defects & feature shortcomings).

You can't control what the product could do in the past. You really can't control what the product has in it today. Past you (or the person who had your job previously) had influence on that. The only thing you can really control is what the product can do in the future.

Make sure when you're presenting to customers that you tease the future. Not in a deceitful way, but in a realistic way. Remember back when we could go to restaurants? Have you ever been to a fancy one and heard how they describe the food?

You don't get 'chicken kebab', you get "Succulent pieces of boneless chicken marinated in ginger and garlic, spiced with freshly pounded black peppercorns, gram flour and chargrilled with beaten egg yolk." (https://www.posist.com/restaurant-times/resources/menu-descriptions.html)

Part of your job is to generate anticipation of an imagined future.

It's not hard to tap into the past, present and future on customer calls, especially in roadmap sessions.

First, tap into the past by showing a quick update of what you've delivered over the past 3-6 months. Sprinkle in an analyst report or two and you've established your team's credibility to deliver. People need to be reminded about 'what have you done for me lately?'. This covers the past and the present. What has been and what is.

Next go into your near-term roadmap. This should include the near-term features and capabilities you're working on. While these may change somewhat, this should be a fairly accurate representation of the future. Customers should be able to see how these specific additions to the product can help them solve concrete issues today. This covers the present and near-future. What is being worked on and what will be done soon.

Finally, tap into the product vision. Here's where you get to let your imagination run free. Think outside the box. Where do you see your product in 2, 3, even 5 years from now?

You're not only showing them where you may go. You're showing them where *they* may go. You're also showing them that you're thinking about the future, not just about what's right in front of you.

People buy not just on what's there, but about where it's going.

Customers want to be heard

5 Seconds- Don't rush to solve the customer problem. First, seek to understand.

It's so obvious when you're on the customer side of this, but very hard to remember when actually talking to a customer. You want to be heard. You want to be understood. You read about this in relationship books and blogs. Don't try to solve the problem immediately. Chances are, you'll try to solve the wrong thing.

Seek to understand.

It's ok to end a call without solving the customer's problem. It's not ok for the customer to feel like you didn't hear them.

I recently was on the customer side of this situation. A vendor was giving me a demo of their product management tool. It was quite impressive. I liked it. They asked me what I thought of it. Considering I've seen a ton of these tools, I feel I'm in a good position to provide feedback. I said "I want the ability to have per-board prioritizations." In every tool I've seen, prioritization is global. If I change the ranking of features in one place, it changes the ranking everywhere. I want the ability to have a 'master' ranking and then on every view, I want to be able to either have a local ranking or inherit from the master ranking.

Instead of asking me for more details or digging deeper, they immediately jumped to a solution already built into their tool. It wasn't bad, but definitely not as robust as what I had in mind.

I felt like these guys had missed an opportunity. I'm perfectly content if they really understood what I was suggesting and decided not to build it. But it never felt like they really got it.

It's so easy to be so proud of your baby. You want to brag about it. You want to show it off. It's tough to hear about limitations. It's mentally taxing to realize there is one more thing to add to the backlog. It feels so good to be able to tell a customer "That problem you're having...we already have a solution for it." Be careful of that mentality.

Better to listen than to tell.

Section X: Working with the C-Suite

5 Seconds- The CxO's of your company are busier than you can imagine and have to make more decisions than you realize. Make their life easier by being succinct and prepared.

Depending on the size of your company, you may have quite a bit of interaction with your C-suite. If you're at a company of a hundred or fewer, you'll definitely have meetings & interaction. If you're at a public company with thousands of employees, you'll have less face time with the company executives. Regardless, this information can apply to Directors, VP's or other high ranking people in your company.

The biggest takeaway is to know your audience and what they care about. At some level, everyone cares about the product and whether it's hitting its stride in the market, but the specifics of what each CxO cares about differ.

Fundamentally, these people need you to do the hard work of distilling the complex into the digestible. If the 5-second rule ever mattered, it's with these folks. For those of you who went to business school or have worked in other parts of a company before jumping into Product, you may want to skip this section.

Not every company will have each of these titles, but *someone* will be in charge of each of these areas of responsibility, even if that someone is taking on multiple roles or they have a title of Vice President or Director.

CEO

5 Seconds- This is the head of your company. Even in a 'product-first' company, this person has more on their plate than you realize.

As President Eisenhower said "The buck stops here". The CEO is responsible for the entire organization. Everyone reports up to him/her.

The CEO sets the company strategy. They set the direction for the company to follow.

This person may have been the first de facto product manager at the company back when it was 5 people in a garage.

CPO- Chief Product Officer

5 Seconds- Keeper of the product vision.

If you follow your org chart and keep looking at your boss's boss and then to their boss, you'll likely report up to the CPO. If your company isn't big enough, the top product person may report a Director or VP of Product. The job is similar even if the seniority is different.

In a single-product early stage start-up, this role may be titled "Head of Product" or even "Product Manager". As a company grows in size and in the number of products offered, the CPO is responsible for the overall product strategy in order to meet the goals set out in the company strategy. They ensure that each of the products is filling the right market need. They adjust the investment in each product. At many companies, the founder of the company was the original CPO, even if they didn't have that title. Once their responsibilities became unmanageable, they hired on someone to take the Product role and the founder became the CEO or President.

Sometimes this role encompases all of the product development organization, including product managers *and* engineering, sometimes not.

The CPO is in charge of delivering quality products to customers and the sales team. They've moved on from managing a single product to managing a suite of products. If you think you're juggling too many balls with your single product, the CPO has to juggle the needs of multiple products.

This person understands the challenges of PM's. They've been there and done that. Use their experience. Let them teach you.

CFO- Chief Financial Officer

5 Seconds- They care about the money.

The CFO is responsible for paying the bills. They make sure there's enough cash in the bank. They're continually running the numbers to make sure the expected money coming in will cover the expenses of running the company.

If you need money for something, you're going to be talking to someone under the CFO. At this stage in your career, you're not going to have any independent budget, but you still may need to make the case for some money from your boss. Understanding the concerns of the CFO *may* help you get that money.

Remember, everyone is coming to the CFO saying they need more cash. They need to hire more people. They need to buy this new application or pay for software licenses. Everyone has a good case, but not everyone gets what they want. Why? Because there's limited funds and each dollar spent needs to make the most return possible for the company.

So when you're asking for money, make sure to frame it in terms of the benefit to the company. How will this extra spend make (or save) the company money?

The CFO typically doesn't care about the product roadmap. They care about the number of people working on the product (i.e. the company investment in your product) and they care about the future revenue of sales (i.e. the benefit the product brings to the company).

CRO- Chief Revenue Officer

5 Seconds- This is your head of sales. They're building a sales machine that only somewhat relies on your product.

Not every company has a CRO, but every company has someone in charge of sales. This person is responsible for generating as much revenue as the company can handle. Their job is two-fold. First, it's to get in front of customers and make the sale. Second, it's to build a sales organization that is capable of scaling. These are two very different responsibilities. At a startup, one person may handle both responsibilities. As you get to larger organizations, the CRO's job is to lead the sales organization.

The CRO wants to make sure the Product organization is building a better mousetrap. The better the product is, the easier it is to sell. Because their people are in front of customers every day, they may have very strong opinions on the gaps in the product. Use their input, but be careful. Sales may chase customers. They want to close deals. That's what they're incented to do. Their job isn't to maintain the product vision. Their job is to maximize revenue.

CCO- Chief Customer Officer

5 Seconds- This person is responsible for all things customer related *after* the sale.

While the CRO is responsible for the account managers and sales reps, the CCO is responsible for the rest of the customer interaction including Support, Technical Support, Training, etc.

The CCO is responsible for creating the bear-hug of customer experience. The way a customer feels about a company is so much more than their experience with the software product. It's wrapped up in their personal interactions with the company representatives. If you're building a complex B2B tool, you may need a strong training program to help new customers understand how to use your product. Customers will inevitably have problems. How does your company respond? What's your Customer Support like? When there's a problem, how does your company respond? That's the CCO's area of responsibility.

CxO- Chief <insert title here> Officer

5 Seconds- There's a slew of possible C-Suite positions.

The C-Suite can be populated by a variety of titles. The ones previously listed are the ones I think you have the highest likelihood of interacting with. Do a quick Google search and you can find many more. Here's an incomplete list of C-level titles. Defining each of these and how they may relate to your job is a bit outside the scope of this book.

- Chief Operating Officer
- Chief Information Officer
- Chief Technology Officer
- Chief Marketing Officer
- Chief Legal Officer
- Chief Security Officer

Section XI: General Good Things to Know

5 Seconds- This is a hodgepodge of other things that didn't fit into the other sections.

The essays in this section are less actionable than many of the other essays. There's not a cohesive theme to this section other than this is what I wish I could have internalized ten years ago.

The Whole Product

5 Seconds- We often think of the 'product' as the bundle of bits that a customer uses. The 'whole product' is not just the bits. It's the bits...and everything else. Support, documentation, marketing, etc.

I remember the first time I heard the term "whole product". I was talking to our VP of Engineering and he was coaching me about the whole product. I was so confused. I thought we were playing a game of "Who's on First". He kept saying I needed to think of the whole product and I kept telling him, I *am* thinking of the whole product and would then show him my roadmap of all the features I wanted to build.

Eventually he beat it into my head.

Some software is so intuitive you don't need instructions. Most isn't. The User Guide is part of the whole product.

Some customers never need to contact your Support Desk. Most do. That Support Desk experience is part of the whole product.

Think of the whole product as the entire customer experience.

What is their purchasing experience? Can we make that better?

Do they need to migrate from another product? How can you reduce that friction?

How do they find answers to questions? Documentation? A chat box on your site? Something else?

This analogy may be a bit of a stretch, but here goes. If your product can be thought of as the travel time between two destinations, then the whole product can be thought of as the actual time it takes from deciding to leave, to actually arriving.

Google Maps gives you drive time. That's analogous to the software customers purchase. It fails to account for the time to 1) load the car, 2) get everyone buckled in, 3) get the kid out so he can use the bathroom one last time, 4) stop for gas and let the kid run around, 5) stop again for another bathroom break, 6) look for parking at your destination.

The typical product approach is somewhat limited in scope (even if it's a huge scope). Understanding that there's more to a whole product than just the work that engineering puts into it will give you empathy for other parts of your organization and help you understand why you may be pulled into these areas.

If it hurts, do it more

5 Seconds- Lean into the tough things. Avoiding pain just delays it. To beat pain, beat it down.

We all have pain-avoidance tendencies. Even from an early age, we're taught to avoid pain.

"It hurts when I touch it"

"Then don't touch it"

This advice may be great when talking to a kid about touching a hot stove. It's horrible advice in a professional organization.

The whole move towards Continuous Delivery was spawned by this mantra of 'if it hurts, do it more.'

Historically, releasing software was a painful process. Companies would release annually, or maybe as often as quarterly. That meant individuals and teams could work in relative isolation for months with the feeling of progress. Then, near the release date, everyone would have to check in their code. You'd spend days or weeks dealing with merge conflicts. Getting the whole thing to build was a challenge. Then QA would come in and start testing. They'd inevitably find bugs. Feature work would stop and everyone would shift to fixing defects. Some of those defects were introduced months ago, but no one knew about them because the code wasn't able to be tested back then. Eventually, the code would be in a releasable state. Now, comes the release. Your release engineers would painstakingly package up your product for various platforms and push it out to your download site or app store.

So what's the solution to this? Some may say, release *less* often. Reduce the pain. But that's the wrong approach.

What people figured out is the best answer is to release more often. Smaller batch sizes reduce risk. There's fewer merge conflicts. Bugs are caught faster. Everyone is happier.

The best software companies in the world are able to push new versions of their product out multiple times a day. The pain drove them to do it better.

This is just one example of If it Hurts, Do It More.

Is it difficult giving quarterly roadmap presentations? Then do it monthly or weekly. Fewer things will change and your audience will get the updates sooner.

Do you struggle in customer discovery meetings? Schedule more of them. You'll get more comfortable and learn how to ask better questions.

Do you get overwhelmed when looking at your backlog? Schedule 30 minutes at the start of every day to dig into it. Take it in bite-sized chunks instead of letting it fester.

There's good evidence that in order to be your best self, you should focus on your strengths and not your weaknesses. I realize that If It Hurts, Do It More focuses on weakness. The point here is to shore up your weaknesses to the point of competency. Once it stops hurting, you don't need to go further.

Don't let your fear of pain hold you back. Push through it. Face it and overcome it.

At best, you're the second smartest person in the room

5 Seconds- Everyone knows more about their specialty than you. Your job is to make sure they're the only one.

PM's are the hub of a company. You sit between Sales, Engineering, Customer Support, Technical Pre-Sales, Finance, and the list goes on. Sales knows more about the specific customer than you do. Engineering knows more about the code than you do. Finance knows more about the budget than you do.

In every meeting I'm in, I'm typically trying to understand the other side. It means that I always know less than the other party about this particular issue. It's like coming in second in every race. It's my job to ensure that it's a different car winning each time.

You may know less about the underpinnings of the code than engineering, but you better know more about: Customers, Finance, and Customer Support than they do.

You may know less about one particular customer than Sales does, but you better know more about the market and the vision of the product than Sales does.

You may know less about the financial outlook of the company than Finance, but you better know more about what you need to build to get the company on a good trajectory than they do.

You should strive to have the second most knowledge about any particular area in the company. This string of second place finishes will put you in first place. Not that there's some sort of competition, but you'll be able to understand cross-cutting concerns better. You'll be able to build better roadmaps since you'll have a more objective view across all the concerns of the company. Not just one specialized view.

Once I realized that I'm eternally in second when it comes to most any issue in the company helped me get over my imposter syndrome. Overcome may be too strong of a word. Perhaps it allowed me to make peace with it.

More on imposter syndrome later. For now, realize that in this situation, always being in second place is the best way to win.

Take Thinking Days

5 Seconds- Sometimes the best way to get things done is to take a day off work...to do work.

I don't know about you, but my days are packed with meetings. A light day is four hours of meetings. Six and seven hours of meetings is not uncommon. Often these are spaced out with a 30 minute block between calls. I realize that part of my job is to coordinate work and make decisions while in meetings. But there's a part of my job that requires time & thought and writing and documenting. Squeezing that work into 30 minute slots is not productive.

I'm not unique at my company. Many of us in Product realized this was happening. We were falling behind in our work because of all the other demands on our time. What to do?

My boss took action and instituted Thinking Days. This was a day to block our calendar once a month and not come into the office. We had carte blanche to miss our regularly scheduled meetings in order to dig deep on something.

The deal we struck was that only one person could take a Thinking Day on any given day, so that the rest of the team could cover for that person and that you did something tangible during your Thinking Day.

What constitutes 'tangible'?

You could write a blog for the company website. You could document your research on a product. Do competitive analysis. Revamp an outdated process. Think deep about the product vision. The guardrails were pretty wide. The idea though was to have some concrete outcome of your work. Even though it's called a Thinking Day, you can't just stare at the wall and ponder all day.

The results were immediate and positive.

There was something liberating to know that life could go on in meetings without us. But more importantly, we had the space and the time to move boulders instead of scurrying between meetings to move pebbles. One day a month was space to make forward progress on larger initiatives while the other 19 days were primarily spent keeping the monster fed.

Sure people in other departments sarcastically asked us over Slack "So I see you're *thinking* on Friday, huh? So you don't get to think on other days?"

I knew the ribbing was meant in good fun, but after explaining the purpose of the Thinking Days and that we're expected to have some deliverable at the end of the day, the joking would stop and a slight bit of jealousy would seep in. Other people wanted Thinking Days.

My boss didn't ask permission to institute Thinking Days. She let the results speak for her.

The team has shuffled in the years since we started Thinking Days. People have moved on. Others have been promoted and new people have come onboard. It's been too long since I've taken a Thinking Day.

I need to take my own advice and block my calendar.

Although I haven't taken a Thinking Day in some time, I recently instituted the practice on the team I currently manage. The engineers felt they weren't as productive as they'd like. They're in too many meetings. So we created Protected Days for them. They can let the rest of the team know they're taking a Protected Day where they won't be on meetings and are generally unavailable. They can use these days for coding or for deeper investigational work. It's giving them back time for deep work.

I recommend you do the same. Talk to your boss and let them know what you plan to do. Don't ask. Go in with a plan and I bet you'll find more support than you expect. Come back with some great output and you might even find the idea spreads.

Find your superpower and feed it

5 Seconds- You have a superpower, but you have to know what it is and then feed it mercilessly.

So often we focus on our shortcomings. What do I need to be better at? What skills or competencies am I lacking? We focus on the negative and think that's where we need to put our energy.

That way lies madness. Or at least, mediocrity.

Everyone has strengths and weaknesses. Things you're good at and things you could improve upon.

Focus on your strengths. Find your superpower. What sets you apart from everyone else? What makes you special?

That's your superpower. Feed it. Encourage it. Strengthen it.

Are you good at writing? Then send out internal newsletters.

Are you good at speaking? Then find every opportunity to get in front of people to present your ideas.

Sometimes it's something more nuanced. My superpower is analogies. I love them. It's how I think. It's how I get my ideas across without going into the ugly technical details. When I talk, analogies just pop into my head about 90% formed. I used to hold back on them, but I've embraced it. It's part of my persona now.

And I still need to feed my analogy animal. Something happens in my brain when I talk that feeds him. He's alert and at the ready, just waiting to jump into the conversation...and it's great. For some reason he gets a little shy when I write. Perhaps he thinks it will take too long to get the idea out on the page or he's worried he'll go down a path that he could back out of while speaking, but could get trapped in while writing. Regardless, I love him and he makes me better. It's a work in progress.

Why not focus on what I need to improve? There's a ton of books out there about this very topic and they'll give you a better explanation than I can, but ultimately, you'll get vastly better ROI by getting better at what you're already good at.

Chances are you already like what you're good at. That helps.

Here's a contrived example, if you have two skills and you're better than 20% of the population in one skill and better than 80% of the population in the other skill. You can improve either by 10%, which do you choose? If you focus on the lesser skill, you've added 2% (10% x 20%) to your overall skill. if you focus on the greater skill, you've just added 8% (10% x 80%). In this example, you get four times the returns by focusing on your strength.

Improve your shortcomings to the point of minimal competence. If you can't talk in front of a group, you're going to have a hard time as a Product Manager. You'll need to get at least passably comfortable presenting to customers and other company stakeholders. You don't have to raise your public speaking skills to the level of a TED Talk. Chances are, you've got other strengths to focus on.

If you ride a motorcycle, you'll know that they tell you to not look at the obstacle in your way. Look where you want to go, not at the pothole or rock in the road. Turns out that you go in the direction of your focus. It's the same here. If you focus on your shortcomings, that's all you'll see. Focus on your strengths and that's what others will see.

So what's your superpower? What's that thing that gives you an edge? Find it, feed it, grow it, use it.

Anything worth doing is worth doing badly

5 Seconds- Just start. Don't wait for perfection to start. Do it badly and you'll learn what it takes to do it well.

This is one of those quotes that may or may not be a real quote. https://www.insidehighered.com/views/2011/04/08/familiar-misquotations. It's something that you'd find on an inspirational poster from the 80's or 90's.

Like most things here, you can read more (and better) reasons for this quote elsewhere, but you're here now.

Too often we (read "I") get stuck in analysis paralysis. What's the perfect solution? How can we make this solution scale and how can we cover all the edge cases? How can we make sure it's really done 'right'?

Answer: you can't.

There's too many things in life and in product management that you can't think your way out of. You have to dive in and get your hands dirty. That's the learning experience. Starting is winning.

My current company is embarking on 24x7 support to enable us to stand behind our uptime SLA's. We started out as an on-prem software company. It was up to the customers to ensure their servers and the applications were running. No more. We're delivering a cloud product and the onus is on us to ensure uptime.

Shifting company policies and culture is a tough nut to crack. Engineers are worried about being woken up due to an alert and not having the tools or knowledge to fix the problem. There's been heated meetings about how to escalate problems.

When we started down this path, the timeline to get ready was estimated at 9 months. That was entirely too long. After some digging & probing, I figured out that the engineering concerns were about getting a perfect solution first and only then starting up the 24x7 support plan. We were trying to think our way out of the problem.

I worked with my engineering manager to come up with a phased approach where we pretended to have 24x7 support, but scaled back. We started with 8x5. Yes, eight hours a day, five days a week. This is business hours support, but we had pageable alerts and an on-call engineer. In effect, we were doing 24x7, but really badly. Then we moved to 24x5. Same as before, but we let the alerts trigger a page out of office hours. Soon, we'll be at true 24x7 support with engineers on call over the weekends.

Going this route cut the 24x7 roll-out time from 9 months to just over 5 months. We started out badly. I made sure the team knew that starting was the victory. By focusing on the starting line, we got to the finish line sooner and with less FUD (fear, uncertainty and doubt).

I recommend this approach for most things. Just start. Even if it's ugly. Even if you know it's less than ideal. Just start. You'll learn more, do more, and finish more. Doing more bad work puts you on the path to doing more good work.

"I still don't understand"

5 Seconds- It's ok to not understand. It's not ok to pretend you do.

I've been working for my current boss for just about a year. During that time, I cannot count the number of times I've heard her say "I still don't understand." She's said it to me, to engineers, to customers. You give me someone she's worked with and I'll give you someone who's had to explain something twice.

This is the most important lesson she's taught me.

Don't be afraid to say "I still don't understand".

What I love about this little sentence is the word *still*. It means that you've already heard an explanation. The messenger has already delivered the message. As far as the other party is concerned, their part is over. They've conveyed what they (feel that they) needed to. The problem is that a message sent doesn't equal a message received.

And after all this, there's no reason to be afraid of saying "I still don't understand. Can you explain it again?"

It took me some time to get used to this. Both on the receiving end ("but I'm being so clear, why doesn't she get it") and on the giving end ("Don't worry Trevor, it's better to ask again than to realize you don't have all the info after the call"). I have to remember that it's better to walk away with a comprehensive understanding of the situation at hand (even if it means saying I still don't understand) than to put on the appearance of understanding. Whenever I worry about not appearing as smart as I sometimes think I am, I remember these three things:

    1. Saying "I still don't understand" implies confidence

A confident person is more willing to admit what they don't know. There's no shame in not knowing everything. In fact the opposite is true. We've all met the insecure person who wants others to *think* they know everything. I don't want to be that person. There was an Austin NPR segment of [Two Guys on Your Head](http://kut.org/post/imposter-syndrome-and-why-its-hard-make-it-when-you-fake-it) that explained "it's confident people who say 'I don't know'" The confident person will know what they know and will know what they don't know. There's no shame in admitting which is which.

2. Saying "I still don't understand" saves time

Yes, it means the conversation is going to continue. It means that the other person can't move on for a few minutes. But it also means that the information is actually transferred. It means that I will be able to explain the issue to someone else. It means that I'll take 2 more minutes of your time now and save us 30 minutes later (this includes time for setting a meeting, setting the stage during the meeting, loss of time due to context switching, etc). I have to remember this when I'm getting info from someone who's in a hurry. It's one thing to ask for a better (or more thorough) explanation from someone who reports to you, it's another thing to ask it of someone helping out generosity.

3. Saying "I still don't understand" conditions people to give better explanations

I've been conditioned to shorten and condense my explanations in order to get to the meat of it quickly. I've still got a long way to go, but I'm getting better. Again, this saves me time from the multiple back and forths I used to have, but what's really great is that I'm getting others used to this as well. People hear me say things like "explain it like I'm five", "ok, but what does that *mean* for the customer", and "I still don't understand". After a few interactions, they're almost expecting to hear me say this. And the best part is when they work to pre-empt me with better explanations.

So don't be embarrassed to say you don't know. It's funny. With all the technology and tools and automation, at the end of the day, it all boils down to human to human interaction. Building software takes a lot of people generating a lot of code, but none of that matters if we can't transfer our ideas from one squishy bit of grey matter to another.

Section XII: Types of Deliverables

5 Seconds- Your product is more than a bundle of features or capabilities. If that's all you focus on, you're missing the bigger picture.

Features

5 Seconds- Features are the things you like in a product. They help customers do more. They're net-new goodness for the customer.

I don't need to go into much detail about features. If you're in the world of product or software in general, there's an overweight interest in features. Do you have a roadmap for the right ones? Do your features help you achieve your product strategy? Is your product becoming bloated by too many features?

Features, features, features.

You can read many more insightful books, articles and blogs than mine that will tell you all you need to know about features.

One bit of advice is to not get too hung up on whether a feature is defined as a Story, or an Epic, or whatever other issue type you use in your tool of choice. If you're just starting out, you'll find religious wars about whether a stand-alone story can count as a 'feature' or if you have to deliver an Epic for it to be called a feature. At the moment, we're constrained by the tools we use. Jira, CA Agile Central, Pivotal Tracker, Targetprocess, etc. They all have their own nomenclature & structure.

If you're just starting out, your company will have this all figured out for you. They may not *fully* have it figured out, but you're not the person (yet) to figure it out for them. Trust that they know what they're doing for now. If this is all going over your head, don't worry.

At the end of the day, delivering features, prioritizing features, deprecating features, scoping features, etc is what most of the online product management conversations revolve around. Crafting useful & valuable features is a necessary part of your job, but it's not all of it.

Defects

5 Seconds- All software has defects. Everyone understands that. Part of the work is to make the product work as advertised.

Anyone who's spent any time in product will have had this experience.

Customer reports a bug. "The product doesn't do what it's supposed to do."

You take a look and maybe even loop in your engineers and lo and behold, the product works exactly as designed. And yet the customer isn't happy.

"But I want to do <fill in the gap here> and your tool doesn't let me do that. This is a defect that needs to be fixed."

"I hear you, but the tool is doing exactly what it's meant to do. What you're asking for is a new feature to be built."

So what is it? A feature or a defect? In many respects, it doesn't matter. The customer feels your product has a shortcoming that they expect should be there. How you deal with this may depend on your business model. If you have millions of customers that all pay a small amount, one angry customer may not merit a response. If you have a small number of high-paying customers, losing one can be a serious hit to your revenue.

From an ideological standpoint, I think of Defects as situations when the product doesn't work as advertised. This means the final arbiter of whether something is a defect or a feature gap lies primarily with the customer. Your job as a PM is to ensure that what's being advertised reflects reality.

What do I mean "what's being advertised?"

I mean everything the customer interacts with that tells them what your product should do. This includes user docs, marketing materials, website content, in-application guides, etc. What should a reasonable customer believe?

You may have to convince your developers of this. They'll look you square in the face and tell you "but the code is doing exactly what we programmed it to do." That may be true, but if the user docs say the application can do X, Y, and Z, but you've failed to code those capabilities, in my book, that's a defect.

One final note about defects. Remember how I said features provide more goodness to the customer? Fixing defects reduces the badness to customers. If you think of the pros & cons of a given product, features are adding more 'pros'. Fixing defects is analogous to removing 'cons'.

Debt

5 Seconds- Debt (aka Technical Debt) is work done in order to accelerate your future delivery. I like to think of this as an investment that will pay off in the future.

The term technical debt comes from the idea that sometimes in software delivery, you realize that you want to deliver more today than you can with the resources and capacity you have at your disposal. You have a couple choices, you can accept that fact or you can borrow from the future. This borrowing may involve cutting corners in the code or building a framework that you know won't be able to scale, but will suffice for today. At some point, you'll have to revisit this issue, but for now, it's good enough. That may be a great decision since it frees up capacity today to work on other things.

An example of this is auto-scaling your computing power for a cloud tool. Do you spend months on building out auto-scaling when you first release the product? Or do you decide to save that time and build out other features that will generate more customer interest and let engineers manually add capacity when needed? Shiny new features will drum up more business and who cares if you can auto-scale if you don't have enough paying customers? You've just accrued some debt. You borrowed from your future capacity and spent that effort on features you feel will accelerate your sales. This isn't an inherently bad practice, but just like financial debt, you need to be careful.

At some point, you'll find that it's worth it to fix your scaling issue and you'll create some issues on your backlog and prioritize them. These issues are really customer facing features. They're also not defects. What are they? The work needed to build out your auto-scaling is Technical Debt. You're doing this work to save your engineers from the manual task of manually monitoring and adding more CPUs to your application.

Personally, I despise the term Technical Debt. It has all kinds of negative associations and has an implicit assumption that you made a decision in the past that's now come back to haunt you. I prefer to frame this as a technical *investment*. Any work that the team makes that will accelerate their ability to deliver in the future in an investment.

You decide your front-end framework is too kludgy and there's a better alternative. Making that move is a technical investment. The assumption is you'll be able to deliver faster on this new framework. How can this be a 'debt' if the new framework just came out?

You decide to build an automated build and deploy pipeline so that each time your developers commit code, an automated process starts up where the code compiles, tests are run, and the application is updated in the cloud. This automated process will seriously accelerate your team's ability to deliver and as such should be classified as Technical Debt work. But to be clear, you never 'borrowed' from the future here. You're simply making an investment in your future delivery.

Abraham Lincoln is credited with saying "If I had eight hours to chop down a tree, I'd spend the first six hours sharpening my axe." This is the epitome of investing in technical debt work.

The mobile phone giant Nokia failed because they didn't invest in technical debt (https://www.5dvision.com/post/technical-debt-is-a-silent-enemy-of-every-product-team/). As a species, we are notoriously bad about investing for the future, even though we're one of the few species that appreciates there *is* a future worth investing for. If you don't spend time on your technical debt, you'll end up in a death spiral. Everything takes too long to build, so you take shortcuts (i.e. borrow from the future), so your accrued debt piles up...making everything take longer. Rinse and repeat.

Risk

5 Second- Risk is some of the hardest work to classify. It's like insurance. You hate to pay for it, but it can save your company.

Risk work is the work you do to make future problems less bad. When your team tells you they need to spend extra time ensuring your customer passwords are properly encrypted and safely stored, that's risk work. All the great work you do on your amazing roadmap and feature design can be undone by a malicious hacker stealing your customer passwords. Your team needs to account for this work.

Good password encryption & storage isn't a net positive for the customer. It is something that's good for them, but having good encryption isn't why they're going to pick your product over a competitor. It doesn't fall under a defect. Good encryption doesn't help your team work faster in the future (like working on technical debt). So it's a Risk item.

Other types of Risk work include work to achieve SOC 2 Type II or GDPR compliance. I like to think of this work as buying a safe and hiring a security guard. It may cost you something, but it protects you against a potentially company destroying event. And even if the work doesn't completely stop a data breach, it may reduce the severity. As an example, perhaps data is lost, but you've encrypted it, so the hackers only get gibberish. Not great, but better than losing plain-text customer information.

I'd also recommend putting work around operational maturity here. This is stuff like allowing your servers to autoscale under heavy load. It's the ability for servers to auto-restart in case of a crash. It's the work that ensures your site stays up. It's the work that notifies your team if there's a problem. Some people may disagree about whether this type of work is a Risk, a Feature, or a Debt, but regardless of how you classify it, you need to appreciate the importance of investing in this work.

Everything Else

5 Second- Not everything your team does will fit into the above categories...and that's ok.

Don't assume that every bit of work that your team tackles will fit nicely into Feature, Defect, Debt, or Risk. Your team will spend time on proof-of-concept ideas that will get thrown out. You may have investigation tasks where an engineer needs to look into something in order to answer a question.

I can't know all the different flavors of tasks your company will use and there may be many. But these other types of work that take engineers time should be the left-overs. Most of your team's work should be spent on Features, Defect, Risk, and Debt. If it's not, then there's a lot of capacity going towards overhead and that's work that isn't really delivering great value to you or your customers.

Section XIII: The End is just The Beginning

5 Second- Thank you!

Thank you for making it this far.

I hope you have found this to be a useful jumping off point. Product Management is a huge discipline. This book has just scratched the surface of what there is to know. Remember that other people's advice and guidance is what they wish they had known. It's not an objective truth. This book is no different. There's so much more out there that I still need to learn. I have my own blind spots, so when you learn something that conflicts with what you've read here, that's just fine by me. Feel free to let me know.

Niels Bohr said "The opposite of a fact is a falsehood, but the opposite of one profound truth may very well be another profound truth." Go find those opposing truths. Find them by doing or find them by study. You need to do both to be great.

This is not the end of your journey. It's only the beginning. Good luck!

www.ingramcontent.com/pod-product-compliance
Lightning Source LLC
Chambersburg PA
CBHW062108220526
45471CB00010B/3644